RECLAIMING BLACK MANHOOD

RECLAIMING BLACK MANHOOD

by
Aaron Counts and Larry Evans

www.unblind.com

www.akobenseattle.org

Reclaiming Black Manhood
© 2006-2007 by Aaron Counts and Larry Evans
Second Edition, Second Printing

ISBN: 0-9774774-0-1

Published in the United States by
Unblind Communications

in association with the
Akoben Brotherhood

Cover photo by Mark Aplet

DEDICATIONS

To Diane, thank you for your love and support. To mom, there's no one like you and never will be. To Dad, RIP, for being the greatest man I've ever known. To Wes, God has given you the strength within. To Di (RIP) and Linda, for always being there. To Roberto, Alicia & Serena, I am blessed to be your father. To Monica, Germaine, Aysha, Jeremiah & Alexandria, you bring joy to my life. Most of all to God the Creator, your blessings are immeasurable.
--LE

For Robin, the tallest 5-footer ever. Thanks for standing beside me. For Jesse, whose inspirational strength and wisdom too often are overlooked. For Dad, who returned to the essence before he could witness all that he inspired, and Mom because of her courage. And finally for my son Azai, who makes me want to be a better man every day.
--AC

THANKS to those people who make this project possible:

Andre Franklin
Kelly Jefferson
Adolphus Mines III
Dr. George Counts
Joseph Smith
Tafuta Fundisha-Bey
and to Keith Hickman for his work on media stereotypes in the *L.E.N.S. Program*

Thanks also to the original change team of the City of Seattle's Department of Neighborhoods Race and Social Justice Initiative for the idea of funding a project like this, and to Larry Gossett for being the only elected official in this region with the courage and conviction to speak specifically to the plight black men face.

Many thanks to Safe Futures Youth Center for working so diligently as fiscal sponsor.

And lastly, to the millions of black men upon whose shoulders we stand. Your courage and strength make this world a better place. This is a small testament to our untold and unheard stories.

HOW TO USE THIS BOOK

Reclaiming Black Manhood is designed to be used by individuals or groups in both structured and informal settings. Sometimes sessions might be led by a facilitator such as a classroom instructor or group counselor; other times they might be gone through by a single brother sitting at home in his living room.

The point of this book isn't just to get through the sections, but to reflect on what you think in each part. It isn't a test, and there are no right or wrong answers, so be honest with yourself in the way you respond. Give yourself a chance to get into it before you decide the process is boring and say, "This is some B.S.!" We are trying to get **ourselves** as black men to do something that has increasingly become a lost art: **to think**. To think about ourselves and each other; to see our individual and collective situations. We aren't used to doing it, and some may even see it as a "white thang." It is actually a survival thang: We are in crisis. If we want to rise up, we have to sharpen our skills of thinking critically and analytically; we have to ask ourselves some hard questions, and be ready for the answers.

Each section is brief, and can be reviewed in sequence or as a stand-alone supplement to other learning activities you may be doing. In writing this, we learned some new words and ideas, and consulted a dictionary often as we created it. Feel free to keep your dictionary handy as well. In a group setting, the responses may be written down or discussed, but should be shared and processed as a group if and when the participants are comfortable.

Special Additions:

There is a section specifically for younger readers (under age 13), which give a brief overview of many of the concepts included. The intent is not to "dumb down" the ideas we present, but to offer them in an age-appropriate manner. **See page 165.**

Also, we know that many black men are being raised, cared for and loved by black women. There is now a section for those sisters who want to help a loved one with his reclamation. **See page 159.**

RECLAIMING BLACK MANHOOD Table of Contents

TIME TO MAN UP!
Understanding and Facing our Current Crisis

Not to know is bad; not to wish to know is worse.
--Nigerian proverb

Many of us are in denial about, oblivious to, or simply don't want to deal with the crisis we are facing. Maybe it's too painful for us, since many of us feel constantly under attack. Maybe it's our low self-esteem and internalized sense of shame. Maybe we're too caught up, or too busy kicking it to be serious or to think about that which is most important in our lives as individuals and as a people.

So what is the crisis we face?

People have a natural desire to be the best at something—to be "Number 1." We've seen the desire to be tops in sports or the music industry, but everyday black men like us are number 1 at so many things.

Too bad most of these things are killing us.

The statistics we top are in areas such as:

- Incarceration rates
- Academic underachievement and school dropouts
- Unemployment/underemployment
- Crimes against black people (including murder)
- Fatherless children
- Diabetes
- HIV & AIDS
- Kidney failure
- High blood pressure
- Prostate & other forms of cancer
- Heart disease
- Shortened life expectancies

These issues have been the reality for many black men for such a long period of time they have become normal, or the *popular paradigm*. We don't really think about this reality; it just is. But why has this reality become the norm for too many black men and boys? In this book, we'll walk through discussions and activities aimed at answering this question, as well as providing some suggestions on how we can work to change our reality.

Our history could be told through the Egyptian legend of Osiris...

Osiris was one of Egypt's most powerful and kind gods. He was the God of Eternity, and his kingdom included that of the lower gods. Seth was jealous of his great kingdom, and so he locked Osiris in a chest and sent him floating across the sea (*the slave trade*). Osiris' sister Isis searched out and found the chest, returning Osiris to his kingdom. Still scheming, Seth then killed Osiris, tearing his body into pieces and scattering them across the land (*the breaking up of Africans and the African continent due to colonialism*). Using her magic, Isis found and buried each piece, allowing Osiris entry into the afterlife, and giving power to his son Horus (*modern day descendents of Africa*) to rule as the sun god.

We too, need to put together the fragmented pieces of our past, so that we can move forward as powerful and productive men. To do this means to acknowledge our deficits, build on our strengths, and take responsibility for our healing in a culturally relevant manner.

Part 1
CULTURAL IDENTITY

"We are involved in a cultural struggle. Culture is more than your music, dress or the food you eat. Culture is everything you do; it's your lifestyle which results from the way you perceive yourself within the context of the world. A part of our culture should be the successful transition from boyhood to manhood. Our measure of cultural success can be defined as securing a high ratio of boys making this transition. We must develop cultural strategies, changes in our lifestyle, which achieve this objective."

--Jawanza Kunjufu, *Countering the Conspiracy to Destroy Black Boys*

WHO ARE WE?
Finding Our Cultural Identity

Jews, Arabs, Turks, Russians, Finns, Swedes, Czechs, Uzbeks, Macedonians, Estonians, Malayans, Cathayans, Japanese, Sinhalese—one and all planetwide—have a nurturing access to the fullness of their myriad histories; histories that often seem as old as time.
--Randall Robinson, *The Debt: What America Owes to Blacks*

Identity is a sense of who you are as an individual. A cultural identity, then, is a clear picture of how you fit into the larger picture of your ethnic heritage, and how that heritage helps define you. Ideally, it should shape our manhood offering guidelines for developing values, strengths and purpose. For too long in our country, this piece has gone undefined for black Americans. Due to our history in this country we lost our many original cultures, and therefore have been defined in the most demeaning circumstances imaginable. As a result, we have associated many negative images and traits with black manhood. That is our popular paradigm, or norm. It is time to conduct a paradigm shift in how we view ourselves and how we define black manhood. The goal is to move away from this distorted view of ourselves and to view ourselves automatically and instinctively in a positive, proud and powerful way.

List the images you see of black men in our society. Think about TV, movies, magazines, music videos, and the general depiction of black men. Write them below.

_____

_____

_____

In contrast, view the list of black people and their accomplishments on the following pages.

15

BLACK INVENTORS AND THEIR CREATIONS
From the Black Inventions Museum

PAPER (Papyrus)
Ancient Egypt

ALPHABET (Hieroglyphics)
Ancient Egypt

STETHOSCOPE
Imhotep, Ancient Egypt

ELECTRIC LAMP
Lewis H. Latimer & Joseph V. Nichols

TYPE WRITING MACHINE
Lee S. Burridge & Newman R. Marshman

BICYCLE FRAME
Isaac R. Johnson

LANTERN
Michael C. Harney

LETTER (Mail) BOX
Philip B. Downing

KEY (Chain) FASTENER
Fredrick J. Loudin

PENCIL SHARPENER
John Lee Love

HORSESHOE
Oscar E. Brown

RIDING (Horse) SADDLE
William D. Davis

REFRIGERATOR
John Stanard

RANGES (Gas Stove)
Thomas A. Carrington

CLOTHES DRYER
George T. Sampson

EGG BEATER
Willis Johnson

MOP
Thomas W. Stewart

DUST PAN
Lloyd P. Ray

GOLF TEE
George F. Grant

HEATING FURNACE
Alice H. Parker

STAINLESS STEEL SCOURING PADS
Alfred Benjamin

GAMMA ELECTRIC CELL
Henry T. Sampson

FIRE EXTINGUISHER
Thomas J. Martin

IRONING BOARD
Sarah Boone

PHONOGRAPH
Joseph Hunter Dickinson

TELEPHONE TRANSMITTER
Granville T. Woods

FOLDING CHAIR
Charles Randolph Beckley

FOLDING BED
Leonard C. Bailey

GUITAR
Robert F. Flemmings, Jr.

HYDRAULIC SHOCK ABSORBER
Ralph W. Sanderson

LAWN MOWER
John Albert Burr

AUTOMATIC (Transmission) GEAR SHIFT
Richard B. Spikes

TRAFFIC SIGNAL
Garrett A. Morgan

EYE PROTECTOR (Safety Goggles)
Powell Johnson

AIR CONDITIONING UNIT
Frederick M. Jones

PROGRAMMABLE TV RECEIVER
(Remote) CONTROLLERS
Joseph N. Jackson

FOUNTAIN PEN
William B. Purvis

DISPOSABLE SYRINGE
Phil Brooks

URINALYSIS MACHINE
Dewey S.C. Sanderson

ELEVATOR
Alexander Miles

CARBON DIOXIDE LASER FUELS
L.A. Lee & E.E. Baroody

CURTAIN ROD
Samuel R. Scottron

TWO-CYCLE GAS ENGINE
Frederick M. Jones

DOOR (Knob) HOLDING DEVICE
Osbourn Dorsey

CHAMBER COMMODE (Toilet)
Thomas Elkins

BREATHING DEVICE (Gas Mask)
Garrett A. Morgan

STREET SWEEPER
Charles B. Brooks

CHILD'S (Baby) CARRIAGE
William H. Richardson

BRUSH (Hair)
Lyda D. Newman

COMB
Walter H. Sammons

DOUBLE TANK PINCH TRIGGER
PUMP WATER GUN (The Super Soaker)
L.G. Johnson & B.M. D'Andrade

ENVELOPE SEAL
Frank W. Leslie

COIN CHANGER MECHANISM
James A. Bauer

MORTICIAN'S TABLE
Leander M. Coles

HOME SECURITY SYSTEM
Utilizing TV Surveillance
M. Brown & A.L. Brown

AIR SHIP (The Blimp)
John F. Pickering

PROPELLING MEANS FOR
AEROPLANES
James Sloan Adams

HELICOPTER
Paul E. Williams

FLYING LANDING PLATFORM
Peachy Booker

What are your first thoughts after reading this list?

_____

_____

_____

_____

_____

How does your definition of black manhood fit when you compare the first list you wrote with the list of inventors?

_____

_____

_____

_____

_____

How did this happen?

The descendents of American slavery are the only group of people in recorded history with no knowledge of our original place of origin. The tangible elements we lost were the history, land, languages, religions and cultural practices of each of our many specific tribes. Even more devastating was the loss of those intangible elements: self-definition, a sense of belonging, strength, grounding, customs, and values.

The groups mentioned in Brother Robinson's quote at the beginning of this section inherently carry these attributes within their being. There's no serious need for Japanese American men to talk about, or redefine Japanese manhood, for their rich history defines it for them. For better or worse, the same can be said for any other group of people—except black Americans.

What happens when a people grow without this self-concept? It can be replaced with other—often negative—traits. Think about the concepts often associated with us: hustlin', pimpin', bangin' and ballin' among them. How often do you see Chinese American men incorporating pimping into their definition of manhood? Rarely. Similarly, you are not likely to see Jewish American men proclaiming that drug sales, criminal activity or extreme materialism are positive elements of their self-definition. The power of their cultural history allows them the ability to mold themselves after positive images.

Let's look at the role a cultural identity can play in America. List the 5 most important priorities you believe the various groups of men exhibit. (Examples: 1. Sex, 2. Money, 3. Family, 4. God, etc.)

Black	Native American	White	Latino	Asian

1. _____

2. _____

3. _____

4. _____

5. _____

If you thought about it and were honest, these lists probably aren't exactly the same for all of the groups. We aren't saying one is better than another, only that a long, historic sense of culturally defined manhood helps to shape these values.

What do you think should be the top priorities for black men?

1. _____

2. _____

3. _____

4. _____

5. _____

What are your personal priorities or top values as a man?

1. _____

2. _____

3. _____

4. _____

5. _____

A cultural connection with ones original land of origin is a very powerful asset in mental, emotional, and physical health. It acts as the glue that holds a people together. It is no coincidence that Alex Haley chose the name *Roots* for his book. The knowledge of ones specific culture acts as the roots that stabilize, nourish and strengthen a people.

As black Americans we function without this foundation or these roots. As a result, our cultural self-concept continues to be manipulated and distorted—by ourselves as well as others—and often works against us. We are battered about and damaged like a tree without roots. Rather than expending our energy seeking a soft place for this tree to fall, it may be time to establish roots so that we can grow and thrive.

These exercises are not designed for us to develop or continue with a *po' me*, victim mentality. In fact, they are designed to do just the opposite: to increase self-awareness, self-determination, and healing. Since the beginning of time, your people have had a tremendous, positive impact on civilization. Even today, despite the crisis in our communities, it has been written that you are the envy of the world. You are a survivor. No other people in history have been through what your people have. Yet, here you are, reading this curriculum, reflecting on yourself, redefining yourself as a black man. Regardless of what current circumstance you find yourself, remember: you are a remarkable human being, and you come from a remarkable people.

PLAYERS AND HATERS
Internalized Racism & Self-Hatred

By the time the fool has learned the game, the players have dispersed.
--Ashanti Proverb

Racism has, is, and likely will always be a serious problem in the United States, especially to those on the receiving end. America was built from a value base of white supremacy and class privilege and continues to be maintained as such. However, we need to be aware and honest about certain aspects of racism today. It ain't your grandparent's racism we are dealing with. It is insulting to the legacy of all of our ancestors to be among the first generations of black men who have not only failed to continue moving forward, but in many ways, have taken steps backward.

Strong words, but it is pretty clear that many of us as black men don't understand the mind games that are being waged against us and how we are being played, rather than being the players many of us claim to be. During discussions on racism and bias in America regarding blacks, the conversations normally revolve around the following topics:

Slavery   Jim Crow   Lynching   Segregation   Discrimination   Racial Profiling

It is hard to imagine what it must have been like for our ancestors to have experienced these practices on a daily basis. As inhumane as those practices were, an often overlooked element is our loss of our culture, a distorted, replacement cultural self-concept, and our failure to redefine ourselves based on all of our experiences, trauma, and accomplishments, and diverse African roots (we'll repeat this idea, because we feel that it is crucial to our healing). As we've stated before, this project is about self-responsibility, empowerment and taking control of our own healing. As with any illness—mental, emotional, or physical—we can't get well until we know what is making us sick.

We have been taught subconsciously to hate ourselves—and each other. This hatred, called internalized racism, shapes the way we view ourselves and others like us. Internalized racism (sometimes called internalized self hatred or internalized racial oppression, among other things) is important and we should understand how it affects us.

> *Take a moment to read the Willie Lynch speech "How to Make a Slave" below. The authenticity of this speech's origin has been debated. Its truth in pointing out some of the causes and effects of internalized racism, though, has not.*

Gentlemen, I greet you here on the bank of the James River in the year of our Lord one thousand seven hundred and twelve. First, I shall thank you, the gentlemen of the Colony of Virginia, for bringing me here. I am here to help you solve some of your problems with slaves. Your invitation reached me on my modest plantation in the West Indies where I have experimented with some of the newest and still the oldest methods of control of slaves.

Ancient Rome would envy us if my program were implemented. As our boat sailed south on the James River, named for our illustrious King, whose version of the Bible we cherish, I saw enough to know that your problem is not unique. While Rome used cords of woods as crosses for standing human bodies along its highways in great numbers you are here using the tree and the rope on occasion.

I caught the whiff of a dead slave hanging from a tree a couple of miles back. You are not only losing a valuable stock by hangings, you are having uprisings, slaves are running away, your crops are sometimes left in the fields too long for maximum profit, you suffer occasional fires, your animals are killed.

Gentlemen, you know what your problems are: I do not need to elaborate. I am not here to enumerate your problems, I am here to introduce you to a method of solving them. In my bag here, I have a fool proof method for controlling your Black slaves. I guarantee every one of you that if installed correctly it will control the slaves for at least 300 hundred years. My method is simple. Any member of your family or your overseer can use it.

I have outlined a number of differences among the slaves: and I take these differences and make them bigger. I use fear, distrust, and envy for control purposes. These methods have worked on my modest plantation in the West Indies and it will work throughout the South. Take this simple little list of differences, and think about them.

On top of my list is "Age", but it is there only because it starts with an "A": the second is "Color" or shade, there is intelligence, size, sex, size of plantations, status on plantation, attitude of owners, whether the slave live in the valley, on hill, East, West, North, South, have fine hair, coarse hair, or is tall or short. Now that you have a list of differences, I shall give you an outline of action—but before that I shall assure you that distrust is stronger than trust and envy is stronger than adulation, respect, or admiration.

The Black slave after receiving this indoctrination shall carry on and will become self re-fueling and self generating for hundreds of years, maybe thousands. Don't forget you must pitch the old Black male vs. the young Black male, and the young Black male against the old Black male. You must use the dark skin slaves vs. the light skin slaves and the light skin slaves vs. the dark skin slaves. You must use the female vs. the male, and the male vs. the female. You must also have your white servants and overseers distrust all Blacks, but it is necessary that your slaves trust and depend on us. They must love, respect and trust only us.

Gentlemen, these kits are your keys to control. Use them. Have your wives and children use them, never miss an opportunity. If used intensely for one year, the slaves themselves will remain perpetually distrustful. Thank you, gentlemen.

When a person or group of people are denied basic human rights by others, told that they are inferior and are targets of cruel and inhumane treatment based simply on who and what they are, they begin to view themselves and each other in this manner. The changes to your mind state may be conscious or subconscious; you may be aware or unaware of your shifting self-image. The result is a cultural low self-esteem from which black people collectively suffer. We have been told negative things about ourselves for long enough that on some levels we have begun to believe them, and many of us now see ourselves and others like us the way our tormenters do. You won't hear black people say, "I hate myself because I am inferior. Since you look like me, I hate you too!" As with most behaviors, it is more complicated than that. Some of the more common subconscious examples of how internalized racism plays out among black people are:

- Referring to ourselves and each other as niggas (no other people have embraced the most racist and demeaning term to describe them).
- Putting each other down and referring to each other as ugly based on dark skin, large lips, wide noses or tightly curled (so-called nappy) hair.
- Referring to those physical characteristics associated to whiteness as good or favorable ("good" hair, light-skinned, thin lips, etc.).
- As black men, many of us embrace the characteristic of being cold, inhumane, uncaring, gangster, ruthless or hard.
- Selling drugs to our own people, within our own community.
- Carrying a gun that we will likely use on another black person, and more importantly, living a lifestyle that causes us to feel we need to be strapped.
- Continually on the prowl to beat another black person out of something, also known as "runnin' game" on each other (could be for a woman, money or something else).
- Neglecting our children, or taking out our own frustrations on them through verbal, emotional and physical abuse and neglect.
- Excessive use of alcohol and use of drugs, sexual acting out, and the physical, sexual, and emotional abuse of others.
- Dating/marrying outside our race based on the belief that "there ain't no decent black women/men."
- "Mean-mugging" each other, or instinctively viewing other black men we come in contact with as potential adversaries (enemies).

The lack of humanity, which is really a reflection of how we feel about ourselves, shows itself in how we treat others. We have created heroes out of brothers who are 'gangsta' or embrace an "I don't give a fuck!" mentality, while at the same time looking down on sensitive, caring, or "soft" men. Brothers who are into pimping, gang-banging or drug dealing may deceive themselves or have been deceived into thinking there are special skills that are required to do what they do. The sad reality may be that the main skills needed to engage in one of these destructive activities is the ability to separate from ones own humanity and treat others in an inhumane way; as objects for our benefit. Or in other words, to treat each other the way our enslavers treated us – **internalized racism**.

Think about and write down times in your life when another black man (or woman) has "beat" or "played" you.

_____

_____

Describe how those experiences made you feel?

_____

_____

Think about and write down times in your life where you have "beat" or "played" another black man (or woman).

_____

_____

Now, how did that experience make you feel?

_____

_____

Is there a difference in how you felt when you "got played" as opposed to when you "played" someone else?

_____

_____

Why do you believe there was a difference?

_____

_____

In order to treat others - especially others who have so much shared history with us - in such a fashion, a great deal of self-hatred is required. Some of us have tried to promote the separation of ourselves from our own humanity as a powerful and admired characteristic of black manhood— **being hard**. Think about the following titles or activities and how we, as black men, may try to justify or excuse them within each other and ourselves:

- Gang member
- Pimp
- Player
- Hustler
- Criminal

- Dealing drugs (small- or big-time)
- Extreme materialism
- Hitting or verbally abusing women
- Financially exploiting others

24

Whether we have been involved in any of these activities or not, there may be a part of us that understands and can relate. We allow these activities within our own communities more than any other people do. In some cases we even admire those who engage in them. Often, our justification is, "At least he's gettin' PAID!!" or "They brought it on themselves." While some of this is due to poverty and economic opportunity, there is more to it than that.

What makes it so damaging is that one must dehumanize someone (view as less than a whole person) before making him or her into a victim. We must view them as less than a whole person. For black people, more often than not, the victims of our exploits are also black. The more that other person resembles or represents who and what we are, the easier it is to shoot, slap, stab, steal from, exploit, pimp, or sell drugs to that person. All of us know a brother who is hard like that (or may even be one ourselves). What may really be going on is internalized hatred.

Those that exhibit internalized hatred have been called "modern-day slaves" by some. Read the following list from the website of Stanely "Tookie" Williams (www.tookie.com). Tookie was the co-founder of the Crips street gang, and has been on death row in California since 1981. Despite his work for peace later in his life, he was executed in December 2005. After reading this list, ask yourself, "Am I still a mental slave?"

Modern-Day Slave Traits
1. A modern-day slave will neglect to educate himself, which in turn creates mental slavery. (During slavery, Blacks were prohibited from learning to read or write. So, these days, *everyone* should take advantage of the opportunity to get an education.)
2. A modern-day slave will swindle and commit other crimes against his own people and others instead of helping to break the chains of poverty by earning an honest living.
3. A modern-day slave will perpetuate self-hate through committing violence on people of his same ethnicity, such as black-on-black violence, including murder, which is a form of genocide.
4. A modern-day slave will deal, buy and/or use drugs that will make him and others function as slaves (addicts) to drugs, slaves to misery and slaves to defeat.
5. A modern-day slave will adopt the wicked ways of the slave master, who disrespected and abused women.
6. A modern-day slave will abandon his children – leaving them for someone else to raise – just as the old masters abandoned Black children by selling them off to other slave owners, not caring about their fate.
7. A modern-day slave will foolishly commit crimes that cause him to end up behind bars, incarcerated, in mental and physical bondage.

Take a look at this list and then read it again. Look within yourself for any similarities and eliminate your modern-day slave traits. If you cannot admit to any of the seven signs, you might be in denial. Perhaps asking yourself some questions about self-hating behaviors will make the concept clearer. Write your answers down, but it is up to you if you'd like to share them or keep them private.

1. Do I carry a gun or other weapon?

2. If I were to use a weapon tonight, what would be the most likely reason?

3. If I were to use a weapon would it most likely be against someone who looks like me?

4. If I could get away with it, would I have sex with a friend's wife/girlfriend/partner?

5. Do I use or sell drugs, have I in the past or would I possibly do so in the future?

6. Do I, or have I ever been a member of a gang? If so, why? If not, why not?

7. Have I ever been locked up in youth detention, jail or prison? If so, for what and how long ago?

8. Do I still engage in the activity that got me locked up?

9. Do I consider women bitches or hoes? Do I ever refer to women as such to their face or with my friends?

10. How often do I read (books, newspapers, etc.)?

11. Who are the 5 men I admire/respect the most? Why do I admire them?

12. When I see another black man about my age on the street, do I prepare to greet/acknowledge him or do I tense up and prepare myself in case he "mean-mugs" me? Which am I more likely to expect, and which am I more likely to do?

13. Is there any specific thing I do regularly that generally helps black people?

14. Is there any specific thing I do regularly that generally hurts black people?

Self-reflection and analysis is the act of looking at ourselves - our actions, values, beliefs and attitudes – and being honest about what we see in order to grow, improve and change behaviors. It gives us a chance to lay down the self-hatred and stop living the life of a modern-day slave.

INVISIBLE MEN
Self-Esteem and Being Seen

> **In American culture the most dangerous symbol, the most frightening symbol, for white people, is black men in love. The moment black men love each other, the United States is done for.**
> --David Shields, *Black Planet*

Much has been written over the years about the importance of self-esteem. A healthy self-esteem has been shown to be a valuable ingredient in raising happy children, in maintaining healthy relationships and in aiding individuals in making positive life choices. Without self-esteem, people can lose their sense of strength and power, instead finding only roles as victims.

According to psychologist Nathaniel Branden, self-esteem "is the experience that we are appropriate to life and to the requirements of life. Self-esteem is confidence in our ability to think; confidence in our ability to cope with the basic challenges of life; and confidence in our right to be successful and happy; [It is] the feeling of being worthy."

In the book *Invisible Man*, Ralph Ellison wrote about the life of a black man searching for identity in a society that refuses to see him. The character feels invisible because of the way others react to him; they do not accept his reality and so they live as though he is invisible. This feeling of invisibility permeates many aspects of our lives as black men, attacking our personal power and self-esteem.

> **Can you think of some time in which you've felt invisible; that people couldn't or wouldn't see you or your reality?**

_____

_____

_____

_____

_____

These types of slights have been studied and written about by doctors—who call them *micro-aggressions*. They are subtle, but hostile acts or attitudes and fit a personal history of racial slights or disregard. These acts suggest to us that we are "less-than" other people or groups and they convey a message to "stay in your place."

Again in *Invisible Man*, Ellison writes about our reactions to these slights and the feeling of invisibility. He says that when you live an invisible life like this, "you ache with the need to convince yourself that you do exist in the real world."

In your life, what are some ways that you attempt to exaggerate your visibility or make sure you're seen?

_____

_____

_____

_____

_____

What effects or consequences do those things have on your life?

_____

_____

_____

_____

Listen to the song, "All Falls Down" by Kanye West or read the excerpt below.

Man I promise, I'm so self conscious
That's why you always see me with at least one of my watches
Rollies and Pasha's done drove me crazy
I can't even pronounce nothing, pass that ver-say-see (Versace)!
Then I spent 400 bucks on this
Just to be like nigga you ain't up on this!
And I can't even go to the grocery store
Without some ones that's clean and a shirt with a team
It seems we living the American dream
But the people highest up got the lowest self esteem
The prettiest people do the ugliest things
For the road to riches and diamond rings
We shine because they hate us, floss cause they degrade us

28

We trying to buy back our 40 acres
And for that paper, look how low we'll stoop
Even if you in a Benz, you still a nigga in a coop (coupe)

I say fuck the police, that's how I treat 'em
We buy our way out of jail, but we can't buy freedom
We'll buy a lot of clothes when we don't really need 'em
Things we buy to cover up what's inside
Cause they make us hate ourselves and love they wealth
That's why shorties holler "where the ballers at?"
Drug dealer buy Jordans, crackhead buy crack
And a white man get paid off of all of that
But I ain't even gonna act holier than thou
Cause fuck it, I went to Jacob with 25 thou
Before I had a house and I'd do it again
Cause I wanna be on 106 and Park pushing a Benz
I wanna act ballerific like it's all terrific
I got a couple past due bills, I won't get specific
I got a problem with spending before I get it
We all self conscious I'm just the first to admit it

What is Kanye saying about the actions we take to combat low self-esteem?

_____

_____

_____

_____

In what ways is your self-worth connected to material items?

_____

_____

_____

_____

What is the alternative?

29

According to psychologist Anderson Franklin, there are seven elements that help us remain grounded in our quest to retain personal power. It is our job to understand these elements so that we can effectively and appropriately seek out their fulfillment. Compromising them throws us off course in our journey to be the kind of men we want to be.

Recognition—The power of feeling you are being acknowledged by others.
Being recognized as a person of worth can go a long way in helping us feel proud of the things we do. Historically, when this type of recognition was lacking, Black men often started our own professional organizations and social clubs to support and recognize each other.

Satisfaction—The power of feeling rewarded for what we do.
Reward can come in many forms: financial gain, public acknowledgement, or a sense of purpose. Often, we get caught up looking for this satisfaction from places that may never grant it rather than cultivating the relationships in which we are likely to gain this sense of satisfaction.

Legitimacy—The power of feeling that you belong.
Once we feel recognized and satisfied, we tend to have a general feeling that "this is where I'm supposed to be." We innately tend to look for places we belong (churches, gangs, the act of calling each other "brother" all work towards helping us identify with a group we can be part of).

Validation—The power of feeling that others share your views and values.
Finding like-minded individuals reminds us that we are not alone. We share stories with one another in barbershops and street corners, nod along to the lyrics of the same songs, or discuss the arrival of the next Jordan all in our quest to share common ideas or outlooks.

Respect—The power of feeling that you are being treated as a person of value and worth.
Feeling respected is vital to the process of feeling like somebody. We've often seen the opposite, fights that break out over sometimes trivial things (like stepping on someone's shoes), because they represent disrespect, and make us feel like we're not getting the respect we deserve.

Dignity—The power of feeling that you are a person of value and worth.
Pride may be defined differently by each of us, but it is essential for us to decide what we are proud of within ourselves, and build on those activities or traits.

Identity—The power of feeling comfortable with the way you are and who you are.
Essential to this concept is the idea that we need to define ourselves, rather than have that identity defined for us.

> **If we don't experience these seven elements, low self-esteem can result in some other characteristics in black men. Ask yourself, "Do I engage in some of these practices?"**

1. A tendency to lie habitually
2. Exaggeration regarding our own accomplishments
3. Disregard for acceptable social norms & rules (such as casually jaywalking in traffic)
4. Loud, aggressive behavior in order to draw attention
5. Abuse of women (physical, emotional, sexual)
6. Bullying
7. Sexual Infidelity (on our spouses/partners, as well as the spouses/partners/wives of our friends & relatives)
8. Laughing at, putting down, ridiculing and publicly embarrassing others

R-E-S-P-E-C-T: Many brothers kill & die behind it

When you hear the news report of one brother stabbing another over some trivial amount of money, it is really about respect. Likewise the reason behind a shootout occurring over one brother stepping on another's Jordans—it's not about the shoes, it's about respect. When one brother "mean-mugs" another and violence results, it's about respect. When you think about it, as black men we are willing to go to costly extremes over this thing we call respect.

Refer back to the seven elements presented by Dr. Franklin. It is fair to say that black men may have a difficult time feeling recognized, satisfied, legitimized, validated, respected, dignified, and positively identified by this society. We must also take into consideration the ways that men have historically gained respect in America, and how black men have been restricted in doing so.

Think about it. Throughout history, men felt acknowledged and powerful—they felt like men—in the following ways:

- Owning land
- Providing for and protecting their families
- Serving in the military
- Pursuing specific careers
- Defending self & others
- Owning a business
- Wealth
- Physical strength and athletic ability
- Feelings of being a valued member of society

These are just a few of the ways—right or wrong—that men felt like men throughout America's history. Obviously, for many years, black men were severely restricted and even forbidden from having our needs filled in many of these ways.

Think about respect for a moment. Name an instance in your life where you felt you were seriously disrespected.

What did you do about it?

_____

_____

Was it worth it? Did you feel as if you became a more valued, respected human being? More of a man?

_____

_____

Since many of us haven't felt that respect we felt was due us, we have developed alternative ways of feeling powerful. Unfortunately, because of our distorted sense of self, many of these ways have been detrimental to us and to the state of black people in general. Some examples include:

- Having control over women.
- Being a player/pimp
- Impregnating women
- Out-drinking others
- Having the nicest car
- Wearing flashy clothes
- Being the slickest hustler, thief, con man or criminal
- Taking NO shit
- … and throughout history, the baaadest, craziest, black man was one who would stand up to the white man

Of course, one was considered truly crazy for standing up to white men because for so long in our history, it meant your life was at stake. And though this may have been the most natural reaction, few were willing to do so.

A basic shift is called for

First, we must understand our history as black men, the elements of personal power and how they apply to us, and how we've compensated in seeking respect in alternative ways.

But most importantly, we need to understand that **respect is internally generated.**

I determine my own level of self-respect. Others can not. They may act disrespectful towards me, and I can act accordingly by kicking ass, shooting, or other means, but they DO

NOT determine my level of respect. This is a subtle difference, but a big one. My level of respect as a person is determined by me—not others.

Nobody can define respect for you. You'll have to do that for yourself. Hopefully along your journey to understand what you'll do to earn respect, you will understand that the 22-inch rim-buyin', pimpin', gang-bangin', gun-packin', loud-talkin', Pitbull-ownin' characteristics are distorted concepts of respect based on our own hunger for recognition. Likewise, they are superficial, symbolic, and external elements that have nothing to do with what kind of person you are.

Is this distorted concept of respect worth dying, killing, or sitting in a prison cell for the next 30 years? If you gain nothing else from reading through this book, try to increase your ability to be honest with yourself, about yourself, your actions and your environment. To do so requires the development of wisdom, strength and courage.

ACTION STEPS

Do a cultural inventory. Observe other cultures and learn to recognize the self-definition through strengths, values, and priorities that an intact cultural heritage brings to them. Then, conduct a cultural inventory on yourself. What role does culture—or a lack thereof—play in your life? How do you define yourself as a black man? If you have never done so, this is an excellent opportunity to make a list of those traits to help you heal and change behaviors and priorities.

READ. You'll notice this theme recurring throughout this book. Reading is one of the most powerful activities in which you can engage. It actually develops your brain, exercises your ability to think, and expands knowledge, vocabulary, and writing skills. Most importantly, reading sharpens your critical and analytical thinking skills. Many black boys/men have been programmed to dislike reading. It is your responsibility to develop an appreciation for reading with yourself, and especially your children.

DNA testing. When you are ready, there are now organizations like African Ancestry, that can test your DNA to determine what specific part of Africa your ancestors came from. This testing can be done for each side of your family (mother & father) as long as they are of African descent. This provides specific knowledge of that which was stolen from us 400 years ago.

Visit Africa. Seeing the proud traditions of various African tribes and cultures is a beautiful thing. Africa is a large continent, with over 50 nations and hundreds of independent tribes, cultures and languages. Learning about them will expand your knowledge of your pre-slavery history, and help you define yourself from a powerful and positive position. African people have not forgotten about "those that were taken away," and will often view your visit as a homecoming of sorts. When economics doesn't allow you to visit, take the opportunity to learn from African immigrants. They can tell you so much about the history, life and culture of their place of origin.

Conduct a healing inventory. As you learn our history and the value of culture, begin to compile a healing inventory. Do you struggle with anger and rage? Are you addicted to drugs, alcohol, or cigarettes? Living a scandalous life? Estranged from your children? Struggling with illegal activity and the criminal justice system? Unable to find and/or keep a job? Make a list of all those issues so you will know exactly what you are healing from.

Be a part of a black men's group. This is important for support, acknowledgement, and recognition, as well as individual and collective healing. Be mindful of the type of group you join. This is about us learning to love ourselves. If there is no such group where you are, get some brothers together and start one.

Self-talk. Self-talk is just that—talking to yourself. The goal is to change your thinking to instinctively having a positive, proud, and powerful feeling about black manhood. Self-talk does work. It trains your mind to think differently.

Acknowledgement. Since we don't always receive positive acknowledgement and recognition from society in general, we have to create this among ourselves. When you see a brother or sister, speak to them. This also facilitates healing of the self-hatred we have been taught. It is especially important to speak to our young people who also struggle with the invisibility syndrome.

Reconnect with your children. If you are a father who is estranged from your children, reconnect with them, as Malcolm said, "By any means necessary." A difficult task, but you have to do it. This will not only help your own healing process, but it will be especially powerful for theirs. It will be difficult at times—especially if there has been a history of sexual or physical abuse. We may even want to consult a professional (counselor or otherwise) to help facilitate the process, but brothers, DO THIS. Our failure as fathers may be the most significant of our issues.

Practice self-responsibility. Our approach at the Akoben Brotherhood is all about self-responsibility, healing, and empowerment. Looking at others as the cause of our struggles is easy—almost automatic. To look at our own part in the difficulties we have takes practice and courage. We are a powerful people, so we can do this. After all, internal reflection is how we grow.

Mentor/help another brother. There is a HUGE class gap within the black community. Middle and upper-middle class blacks have left poor black people behind. Connect with a brother who needs it most and bring him along as you take this healing journey. Don't judge the brother, because we all need to heal. Street corners are full of these brothers, so you won't have trouble finding someone.

Understand your priorities and values. Make a list of your priorities as a black man. Money? Women? Your children? Material possessions? Helping our people? Once you make your list, chart the amount of time you spend on those things you say are top priorities, compared to those things we don't want to admit to.

Affection. If you have children, learn to show them affection. Life is hard enough for them; they don't need us acting hard, too. Show care and concern for other children and all of our people. Acknowledge brothers when you see them in the community with their kids. It shouldn't be a big deal to see a brother with his children, but it is too rare. As we recognize each other for being good fathers, ask those you meet to pass this practice on. We too often fail to recognize each other for positive traits. Doing so can be a big step towards redefining manhood.

Self-respect. Develop ways to fill your own needs regarding the seven elements of personal power. Redefine what respect means, and that our level of respect is internally developed, not by external forces. Putting our respect into another person's hands is the most disempowering thing we can do. Claim it for yourself.

Overcome complacency/inaction. One of the most damaging elements of internalized racism is the failure to do anything about our ills. You'll notice many brothers talking about what's wrong, but few willing to take action and actually DO something. This is partly due to centuries of being programmed to turn over control of our lives to external elements, but we can reclaim that power. Rosa Parks died recently. She showed what the courage and action of one person can do. What is our excuse?

Part 2
MEDIA & ENTERTAINMENT

"The media is the most powerful entity on earth…They have the power to make the innocent guilty and to make the guilty innocent, and that's power. Because they control the minds of the masses."

--Malcolm X

THE DISTORTION of OUR SELF-CONCEPT
In Print, Visual & Audio Media

Media distortions and outright reversal of truth used as attacks on the images of certain groups have been historical staples within America's media industry. For example:

- Images of Native Americans portrayed as murderous, scalping, raping savages were commonplace in old western movies, despite the opposite being more reflective of historical fact.

- Images of Japanese as ruthless, diabolical, untrustworthy, murderers in WW II movies, while America remains the only nation to have used weapons of mass destruction--against Japanese civilians by way of two atomic bombs.

- America's indictment of Islam as a religion that spawns terrorism, while America's religious institutions have historically advocated hatred, violence and terrorism toward certain groups of Americans – subtly or blatantly – in "the name of God."

- Promotion of the "freedom and liberty" propaganda to the rest of the world, despite America's history showing great effort to restrict both among many for the vast majority of our history.

- Fear mongering in film, beginning as far back as 1915 in the movie *Birth of a Nation* by D. W. Griffith.   Birth of a Nation was produced to instill fear in white America as to what would happen if blacks received equal rights. Despite its blatant racism, it is often cited as one of the greatest films in American history. Its cinematic legacy continued through the Blaxploitation films of the 1970s and lives today in "gangsta" or "hood" movies and comedies about so-called black life.

Media indoctrination begins early in our lives. Images of ourselves we were once offended by, we are taught to accept and even imitate.

> **Can you recall media images of black people that were once offensive to you, but which you came to accept, or even imitate? What were the images and how did they make you feel?**

_____

_____

_____

_____

_____

While other groups of people have had demeaning images of themselves portrayed in the media, the impact of the damage to blacks is accelerated to another level. Because of our lack of historical roots cultural self-definition, America's media has not only projected demeaning and dehumanizing images <u>about</u> blacks, but also has succeeded in instilling a distorted, self-defeating, internalized self-concept <u>among</u> the descendents of slaves. In other words, we have internalized those images and accepted them as our own.

The so-called "acting black" syndrome

There are now certain behaviors associated with blackness, or "acting black." With the rich history, diverse experiences and accomplishments, and wide range of beliefs among black people it seems fair to assume this concept of acting black is a phenomenon that can only be created and promoted by mass media.

The most damaging element of this phenomenon is how easily we as black people embrace it. The behaviors in question are not behaviors such as academic excellence, social activism, scientific and technological discovery, or strong family life. Sadly, the behaviors associated with blackness are typically superficial, ignorant or obnoxious. Behaviors such as:

- Loudness
- Obscenity
- Natural rhythm
- Athletic ability
- Extravagant, outlandish dress
- Comedic buffoonery
- Overly sexual and/or overly aggressive behavior (black men AND women)
- Misuse and mispronunciation of the English language
- Hard, ruthless, unfeeling behavior
- Pimp-like, abusive, domineering behavior towards women
- Criminal and unethical activities
- Verbal boastfulness combined with incompetent abilities
- Unrealistic exaggeration and habitual lies and dishonesty

In fact, when we see men or women of other races engaged in these specific behaviors, they are often referred to as "acting black." Conversely, book smarts, punctuality, correct grammar and traits such as these are often decried as negative or "white" traits. As an example, we claim President Bill Clinton as the "first black president" due to the fact he plays the saxophone, admitted to smoking weed, and exhibited the uncontrollable, sexual urge to have sex with – as one of many comedians put it – "fat white women."

The low point of the "acting black" phenomenon has to be the use of the word "nigga" as a term of affection or camaraderie (friendship). No other people have taken the most offensive term used toward them, embraced it, and made it the norm. Then again, no other people have spent so long searching for an identity.

Watch scenes from so-called black movies, especially those classified as comedies, like the ones below:

- Friday (as well as its sequels)
- Soul Plane
- Don't be a Menace to South Central
- Another Scary Movie
- Be Cool

Has it gotten to the point that being black comes down to talking slang, holding your Johnson, cussing, smoking weed, drinking "yak" and acting "ghetto?"

Discuss or write down the images of black men – good and bad – you have witnessed in the media)

_____

_____

_____

_____

_____

We repeat, because it's worth repeating, the media might be the most damaging entity to black people in modern society. Among many of us – especially our children – it is in part where values, priorities, self-definition, and distorted identity are developed and maintained.

This is no accident. Advertising, research, and corporate entities spend billions of dollars studying what appeals to us. It then becomes a self-perpetuating form of destruction, since we rarely see any other type of product marketed to us; we are conditioned to believe this is what we should like. We then internalize these images and values, make them profitable, and are given more of the same. Now, even during the rare instances where a movie or show displaying positive images of black people is produced, we will reject it in favor of Soul Plane or its like.

If you do nothing else, teach yourself and your children to view all forms of mainstream media for what they are. They are a tool controlled by corporate America. Since corporate America is predominately white-owned, the products it creates exaggerate the importance and values of whites at the expense of all others. More importantly, though, it treats all of us as consumers, hoping our minds will be numbed into believing what we are told without questioning or analyzing. When that happens, it fulfills its role as a tool for social control.

With the advancement of cable and satellite technology, there are literally hundreds of television channels at ones disposal.

With so much information available and the critical issues black people face, list the number of shows available on television where our issues are discussed in a serious, progressive, and uncensored manner:

_____

_____

_____

_____

_____

If you are completing this in a group, discuss what you came up with.

Here in Seattle as well as other cities around the country, public access channels allow the public to produce and broadcast their own show. Occasionally, a person might find subjects of substance on those grassroots outlets. As for the hundreds of other channels available through the more mainstream media, apart from Tavis Smiley and Tony Brown, there aren't too many others attacking black social issues with any regularity. On the other hand, on most of those channels you would not have a difficult time finding black people in comedic buffoonery, stereotypical athletic images, criminal behavior, sexually exploitive images, extreme materialism, and promoting the "thug" lifestyle. Sadly, you wouldn't have a difficult time finding black actors to fill those roles or black audience members to watch them, either.

Wake up brothers, it's a new day. We need to re-learn to view the media in a completely different way.

WHAT ARE YOU LOOKING AT?

It is dangerous to continue to watch movies or television in the manner in which we have been trained. Actually, trained is the wrong term. Training involves teaching, which implies a teacher and a learner. In this case, the supposed teacher does not construct lessons with the intent of teaching, but relies on deception in order to achieve the desired results. This deception relies on our disinterest or disengagement from a critical thinking process while we interact with the images being presented—Being a passive rather than an active participant.

In America, we like to look at entertainment as a form of escape from our daily lives. We want a way to shut out the world, so we turn our active brains down to simmer, sit in a dark movie theater or living room and invite the images on the screen into our heads. The danger in taking this approach is that in doing so, we trust the creators of the film to have our best interest in mind. Big business controls Hollywood, and the mission of big business is not to protect, educate or inform viewers, but to generate revenue.

The primary concern of movie or television producers is to make money. They do so by selling us a product, that product is movies. Like other industries, the entertainment industry spends millions of dollars on market research and demographic studies. As a result, they essentially, group people together on arbitrary criteria (or stereotypes) like age range or ethnicity or sexual orientation. Someone figured out that doing so would make the studios more money.

These days, health-conscious people rarely consume foods without first identifying the nutritional content of them. The FDA regulates the labeling of food with the stated goal of aiding people to take the proper precautions in their quest to remain healthy. Likewise, if we are striving to remain mentally healthy, we should have an understanding of how our minds and spirits may interact with the items they ingest. In this case, we are talking about the images and information packaged as entertainment.

Some of the questions we should ask ourselves:
- Who created this? What do I know about the history of that person, company, etc.? Could there be a particular agenda involved in making it?

- Is there a clear hero/villain? If so, how are those characters developed (i.e., what makes them heroic/villainous)?

- Do I relate to any characters in particular? Why? Is the portrayal of those characters realistic?

- Do the stories or characters being shown fit with my own personal understanding of the world and my place in it?

THE EVENING NEWS

The world of contemporary news is a world that exists for the VIP's – the very important people. Their everyday lives are what is important; if they get married, if they divorce, if they eat, what clothes they wear or what clothes they take off – these major movie stars & big politicians. But common people only appear for a moment – when they kill someone or when they die. For the communications giants, the others, the excluded, only exist when they are dead, when they are in jail or in court. This cannot go on!

--Subcommandante Marcos, of the EZLN

The EZLN, more often called Zapatistas, are a revolutionary group fighting for freedom and protection for the indigenous tribes of Mexico.

Over the course of a few days, watch the local and national news. Take notice of each time you see a black person. Write down or remember the basic information about the story, what the person did or said, and any other information you think is important. What did you see?

_____

_____

_____

_____

_____

Does the depiction of black men in this country fit with Marcos' description above? How is it the same and/or how is it different?

_____

_____

_____

_____

_____

In their book, ***The Black Image in the White Mind,*** Robert M. Entman & Andrew Rojecki studied television and movie portrayals of black people and characters and published the following findings:

Black defendants are simply treated differently on local television news from their white counterparts.

Examples:

- **Times more likely that a mug shot of the accused will appear in a local television news report when the defendant is black rather than white: 4.**
- **Times more likely that the accused will be shown physically restrained in a local television news report when the defendant is black rather than white: 2.**
- **Times less likely that the name of the accused will be shown on screen in a local television news report when the defendant is black rather than white: 2.**

Network news tends to "ghettoize" blacks. Increasingly, African-Americans appear mostly in crime, sports and entertainment stories. Rarely are blacks shown making contributions to the serious issues of the country.

In a sample of network news:

- **Number of sound bites on foreign affairs uttered by whites: 99. By blacks: 1.**
- **Number of sound bites on economics uttered by whites: 86. By blacks: 1.**
- **Number of sound bites on electoral politics uttered by whites: 79. By blacks: 0.**
- **Number of sound bites on sports and entertainment uttered by whites: 35. By blacks: 11.**
- **Number of sound bites on crime uttered by whites: 40. By blacks: 3.**

We are not providing this information to, once again, show what "they have done to po' us" but rather to provide factual information on how we, as black people, are portrayed through the media. This, subsequently, contributes to how we feel about ourselves. As we stated earlier, we can't properly heal unless we know all of which we need to heal from.

Many of us have had a sense that blacks are portrayed in an unfavorable manner compared to whites. When this is brought up, we are accused of being paranoid, avoiding responsibility, or "playing the race card." This contributes to self-doubt, as you question that which you know to be true.

Exaggerated Importance vs. Marginalized Invisibility

It has often been suspected that America's media enhances the importance of white life, while minimizing the importance of black life. White history has routinely been glorified, while black history has been ignored. White accomplishments have been exaggerated and distorted to their benefit, while black accomplishments have been hidden and distorted to our detriment (damage). There may be no other area where this practice is more evident than America's media. It does damage on multiple levels, including the following:

- Promotes an unearned, inherent sense of white privilege to white people
- Promotes a sense of invisibility to blacks
- Contributes to America's base philosophy of white supremacy
- Consciously and subconsciously contributes to the belief by all that white life has more value and importance than that of other people
- Contributes to an inherent feeling of inferiority, self-hatred, and internalized racism by blacks and other people of color

To be clear, the premature loss of life is always tragic. As black men we are not only called to appreciate the worth of black life, but to value all life. We must not fall victim to believing the lives of some are more important than others, as the news might promote. Think about the coverage of Hurricane Katrina's black victims and white heroes, or the exaggerated importance of Laci Peterson's murder. Ask yourself how coverage might be different—if it existed at all—for victims belonging to another group.

We need to be very wary and suspicious any time we see ourselves presented in the media. Some of our favorite shows prove our acceptance of demeaning images of ourselves. These programs include talk shows like Maury Povich or Jerry Springer, most television court shows, and that embarrassment we call "our" network—BET. These are all blatant examples of how we have come to accept the humiliation.

From the constant images of us as comedic buffoons, materialistic rappers, simplistic athletes or dangerous thugs, we must begin to see the media in a different light. We must also understand that America's media is ratings-driven, so each and every television show, news broadcast, movie, and advertisement is designed to appeal to the largest audience possible. Therefore, black people are portrayed in a manner that is comfortable for the majority of Americans. If a show or newscast is designed with the best interests of black people in mind, it may not appeal to the majority of consumers, and remember—the bottom line is money.

So, cut back on the television, movies, videos, violent video games, and DVDs. Statistically, blacks have been shown to watch more television than other racial or ethnic groups. Why? Recent studies have shown that children under 3 years of age would benefit from watching NO television. When you do choose to watch or listen, be more selective. Teach yourselves and your children to interpret the media with a critical, skeptical eye. Show them how advertisers target and manipulate them, and why you and your family will not abide by this manipulation. Develop alternatives to the consumption of media as our only forms of entertainment; read, and pass that love on to your kids. Most importantly, since it is unrealistic to expect us to avoid television and movies altogether, remember to keep your brains active while you watch, discussing what you're seeing and hearing.

THE MANDINGO SYNDROME
And Black Athletes

If you ever get the opportunity to do so, view the 1970's era movie **Mandingo** with ex-heavyweight boxer Ken Norton. The movie, in true Hollywood tradition, bastardized and misrepresented the name of the proud Mandinka people of West Africa—a confusion we want to avoid here. In the film, Mandingos are portrayed as *superslaves*, used for breeding physically superior slaves. Wealthy whites travel from afar to watch as plantation owners pit their Mandingo against one from another plantation in physical combat, as others place wagers on the bouts.

In the movie, Mandingos often lived separate from other slaves, having a higher standard of living. Encouraged to maintain distance from the other—more common—slaves, they performed for the entertainment of their owners and other wealthy whites. The special treatment they received isolated them from other slaves, and produced a loyalty to the owner, despite being viewed as mindless beasts, physical specimens, thoroughbreds and studs.

> **Think of modern-day professional black athletes in the same categories. Do any of the same rules seem similar? What examples are you able to come up with?**

_____

_____

_____

_____

_____

> **Following is a summary from chapter 2 of the book, *Invisible Man,* written by Ralph Ellison:**

A young man graduating from high school gives a speech at his graduation. Following the ceremony, he is invited to present his speech to the power brokers in the town (the character's name is never stated in the book, so we call him the Invisible Man from the books title). After arriving at the best hotel in town where the men have gathered to hear his speech, Invisible Man is compelled to participate in an initiatory battle royal, in which a group of young black men from the town are forced to fight each other until there is one winner.

Before the actual boxing match, the powerful men at the gathering parade in front of the young men a naked white woman who has a tattoo of the flag of the United States on her stomach. Some of the white men insist that the black youths look at the woman while others insist that the youths refuse to look. This situation creates a state of havoc, and then the battle royal begins. The Invisible Man along with nine other young black men from the town are blindfolded and are forced to fight each other until there is one winner. It is clear that if they don't fight each other, they'll have to fight the white men in the room.

Following the fight, coins are thrown onto a rug, and the young men fight each other to grab the money. When they touch the coins, they find that the rug is electrified and they receive a shock from the metal coin. The white men laugh and cheer them on. Once the episode is over, they learn that the coins are not gold after all, but merely fakes used to advertise a local car dealership. Swallowing blood and sweating from his battle, Invisible Man finally is able to deliver his speech. He is rewarded with a scholarship to the segregated state college for black students.

In what ways is the scene similar to the black man's experience in the entertainment or sports industries?

_____

_____

_____

_____

_____

_____

_____

To be fair, the bias of media coverage we discussed also applies to professional athletes. Negative stories involving these individuals are widely publicized, while the positive, socially conscious acts are downplayed or hidden as if to avoid promoting a positive trend among black athletes. For example:

Did you know:

- Ex-Chicago Bears defensive end Richard Dent spent thousands of dollars to convert an abandoned, inner-city hospital into a community center for at-risk youth in inner-city Chicago.
- Atlanta Falcons running back Warrick Dunn started a foundation that has purchased over fifty fully furnished homes for single mothers, in honor of his own mother, a deputy sheriff who was murdered in a store robbery.

- Houston Rockets center Dikembe Mutumbo has spent over 12 million dollars to build a hospital in his homeland of Nigeria.
- Tampa Bay Buccaneers linebacker Derrick Brooks "adopted" a whole classroom of inner-city elementary school children, promising to pay their way through college if they maintain school attendance? These children can contact him throughout the year, and he routinely takes them on outings.
- Ex-Seattle Mariner second baseman Harold Reynolds spent $25,000.00 of his own money to promote a youth baseball league to attract more inner-city Seattle youth to play little league baseball. The Mariners suggested he not do so in the future as "those people" don't buy season tickets, advertising or luxury boxes.
- Ex-Houston Rockets great Hakeem Olajuwon refused a multi-million dollar "Jordan-like" contract from Nike, due to the high cost of their shoes and instances of youth killing each other over them.

Those are but a few of the positive, yet little-known acts many professional athletes perform. Despite talk of role models, one can't help but wonder if professional athletics—and America—really want black athletes to be more conscientious. If the brothers did so, it could have a devastating impact on the sports industry, and the American economy.

Who are your favorite athletes?

_____

_____

_____

Why are they your favorites?

_____

_____

_____

Think of the tremendous impact the following individuals had on sport – and society:

- Muhammad Ali
- Jackie Robinson
- Arther Ashe
- John Carlos
- Tommie Smith

- Jim Brown
- Hank Aaron
- Carl Eller
- Magic Johnson
- Kareem Abdul Jabbar

- Kellen Winslow
- John Thompson
- Jack Johnson
- Jesse Owens

In the past, black athletes routinely contributed to the social, political and racial progress of black people. It should be noted that when many of the above-named brothers were active in their sports and social movements, they were routinely hated and threatened. Their quest for dollars didn't stand in the way of their social consciousness, however.

Role change

The role of sports has changed among black people in recent years. The media has had a significant role in this change. Today…

- Due to the disproportionate media exposure of black athletes compared with other lines of work, and the large sums of money, far too many black boys aspire to be professional athletes.
- Also due to their high visibility, when today's black athletes run afoul of the law, it receives exaggerated, disproportionate media attention.
- As is the case with black people in general, today's black athlete is lacking in social and political consciousness compared with black athletes of the past.
- The media chooses to focus the most attention on the flamboyant, antisocial, materialistic, superficial and illegal acts of black athletes, while minimizing or ignoring those acts that show these athletes in a more complete, conscious light.
- Because of the lure of huge endorsement contracts, many black athletes avoid taking a position on political or social issues for fear of damaging their marketability.
- As black people, many of us vicariously live out our own failed dreams and aspirations through athletes and athletic teams, starting with our own children and the distorted importance we place on athletics in their lives.

Although the media plays a significant role in this exaggerated importance of athletics among our people, we are primarily responsible. There are ways in which we can reverse this damaging trend:

- Limit our obsession with sports and athletics.
- Understand ourselves, and teach our children that the exaggerated emphasis on athletics keeps us from achieving in other areas—by design.
- Place more importance on, attend, and support other events by our children, and within our community (academics, music, arts, social and political activism, etc.).
- As coaches, teachers, parents, and school administrators, black men are directly responsible for the exaggerated emphasis and high priority given to athletics above all else.
- If you are a coach, develop the whole person, not only the athlete.
- Participate in martial arts, yoga, meditation, and other non-competitive forms of exercise.

We aren't advocating the elimination of enjoyment, leisure activity, relaxation, and competitive fun. We simply seek to decrease the exploitation and manipulation of our people.

MODERN-DAY MINSTRELS

Minstrel shows began in the U.S. in the 1830s, with working class white men dressing up as plantation slaves. These men imitated black musical and dance forms, combining the public's interest in black culture with savage parody. By the Civil War the minstrel show had become a world famous and respected form of entertainment. Late in his life Mark Twain fondly remembered the comic darkies and rousing song and dance of the "old time nigger show." Some of America's most famous historical songs—like *Dixie, Camptown Races,* and *Oh Susannah*—began as minstrel songs. America's first talking picture, *The Jazz Singer* (1927), was a blackface movie in the minstrel tradition.

The minstrel show tradition began with white men using burnt cork or greasepaint to blacken their faces, dressing in wild and colorful costumes, and performing songs and skits that mocked African Americans. After the Civil War, black men could appear in minstrel shows, and several of the most famous minstrels were black men who wore makeup and portrayed white men imitating black men. Their satire was just as biting and stereotypical as that of the whites.

There were several stock characters that reappeared in the minstrel shows, most notorious were "Jim Crow," who was a stereotypical carefree slave and "Zip Coon," who was a free man famous for putting on airs or boasting. The parody in minstrel shows was often savage.

Minstrel shows continued to be popular well into the 1950s, and highschools, fraternities and local theater groups would often perform minstrel shows in blackface. As black Americans asserted their political power, these portrayals became less accepted, but did the minstrel show go away?

Images common to that past era are still perpetuated by comedians, actors and musicians today. Compare:

51

Think about the portrayal of black men in music, television and movies (or compare those pictures above). Do you notice any similarities to the demeaning images from the past?

_____

_____

_____

Can you think of instances of black entertainers who exaggerate stereotypes of black culture for a largely white audience? Is this a form of minstrel show?

_____

_____

_____

What about white artists imitating black artistic or cultural forms? Think about white rappers, blues-inspired rock music, dancers, etc. Are they expressing admiration of the culture or just stealing the art form?

_____

_____

_____

During your life, are there any images of black men in the media that influenced your behavior?

_____

_____

_____

Name some negative images of black men you recall seeing in the media.

_____

_____

_____

Another portrayal of black men that has become commonplace is of the brother who talks a good game but has nothing to back it up. These brothers can be described as being "all bark, but no bite," often portrayed as loud, boisterous, belligerent, habitual liars and constantly bragging. Some of the common subjects they exaggerate about are:

- Popularity, control, persuasiveness, and sexual exploits with women
- Talents, expertise and abilities
- Knowledge on all subject matter
- Toughness, courage and ability to fight

- Money and material possessions

Ironically, these brothers tend to be the only ones who are not aware of their ineptness. The reality for these brothers is usually:

- Offensiveness, poor social skills and avoided by women
- No identifiable talents to speak of - often portrayed as generally incompetent
- Noticeable ignorance of all they claim to be masters of
- Cowardly, weak and not very intelligent
- Chronic liars who have little to show for themselves in life

Sadly, such images of impotent, lying, loud black men have become commonplace. The "style without substance" dynamic is a staple in the media. From JJ of "Good Times," George Jefferson in "All in the Family" and "The Jeffersons" to various characters played by actors Anthony Anderson ("Barbershop" and "Romeo Must Die") or Chris Tucker ("Rush Hour" 1 and 2), these images have become so common, we laugh at them along with everyone else.

With the number of critical issues we face as black men, we can't afford the constant comedic release. Again, there is nothing wrong with a sense of humor, and laughter is good for ones health. But we have become so well known as class clowns, comedians, partying people and fun lovers many of us have forgotten how to be serious. This has to change.

ACTION STEPS

DDD—Drastically Decrease the Damage. Simply put, we have to shut the television off, rent fewer videos and DVDs, go to fewer movies, and cut down on the video games—especially the violent ones. Although we may be grown, the media still inflicts damage upon us by altering our self-concept and working to increase our consumerism. We pass these values—good and bad—on to future generations. Our children will do what we do, not what we say, and the media does untold damage to their minds and self-concepts.

Again, READ. Read a book, the newspaper, alternative and/or ethnic papers that give a more complete picture of current events than taking the word of one source. If you have a computer, or can access one at the library, there are countless online sites that print news and stories worth reading. Reading is one of the most powerful things we can do.

Create a love of books in our children. We should read to our children from birth—even before birth. May sound strange but reading to infants helps develop their brains. Children are capable of reading before they begin school, we just don't take the time to teach them. A book is among the best ways to help a young mind grow, but a bookstore in our community is often a lonely and empty place. (I have a friend who has a son who's now grown. He didn't buy his son many toys, and no video games. When his son misbehaved, my friend took his books away. This young man learned to value his books above all else. Manipulative, but it's better than letting the media do it. By the way, that young man is brilliant, breezed through school, and has more awareness and black consciousness than most people I know.)

Learn & teach others to view media critically. Television can be a good learning tool when used sparingly. The Discovery Channel, PBS, History Channel, and other documentaries often have some very educational shows. We also need to learn (and teach our children) how to study the media from a critical and analytical perspective. By keeping our minds active while we watch or listen, we can learn so much about ourselves and our world. When we discuss what we're seeing and hearing, we not only take some of the power away from these media outlets, but we teach our children untold lessons about who they are, too.

Put athletics in their proper perspective. We are now aware that many young brothers who don't aspire to be rap stars still believe they'll someday be in the NBA or NFL. The exaggerated emphasis on sports among our people has reached insane proportions. We need to expose our youth to black inventors (remember your list?), scientists, artists, engineers, activists, and others. It's not enough to tell them about these people, we need to enroll them in programs. Help them spend half the time actually learning to play an instrument, paint, write poetry, or engage in social activism as they do playing basketball. But before we can do this with our children, we need to hold these values ourselves.

Identify/support socially conscious athletes. The media will focus on the flamboyant, self-promoting athletes such as T.O., Dennis Rodman, and Randy Moss. Nothing against those brothers, but we need to be aware of those brothers and sisters who were bigger than their sport—Muhammad Ali, Arthur Ashe, Warrick Dunn, John Carlos and Jackie Robinson. Seek out and highlight the stories of modern-day athletes and celebrities who exhibit social consciousness and action. Doing so will let your kids know where your values lie, and can even impact the type of coverage those athletes receive.

Recognize past/modern day minstrels. Watch some of the old images of Stepin Fetchit, Amos and Andy, Jim Crow, and some of the other early images of black men. Then watch modern day images of black men in comedic roles. Anthony Anderson, Chris Tucker, Martin Lawrence, Jimmy Walker, the younger Wayans brothers, and too many others. Define the similarities. If you have children, show them the comparisons. Help them (and yourself) to understand that the hustlin', jivin', slick, smack-talkin' brother is nothing new, and is a role designed for us by others.

Other Steps

If you want to take some serious action, you can write to the executives at various stations to let them know of your displeasure with the insulting images of black people. Also, stop purchasing the products advertised on these shows, and write to the corporate entities that make them to let them know of your boycott.

It is important to inform the masses of our people about the damage the media is doing to us. At school, the barbershop, church, the gym, and any other place you find yourself among our people, begin having these conversations. Instead of talking about sex, sports teams, or the latest rap, we need to begin having serious and informative discussions.

Contact and support those athletes, entertainers, and other public figures who do have a level of social consciousness. Many athletes and entertainers are subtly encouraged to be obnoxious, self-promoting, and ignorant. Conversely, when they take a stand on a social issue, they are often attacked by mainstream America. If we don't support those who try to display a level of consciousness, why should they continue? Remember, they have a need to heal and re-educate themselves also - whether they realize it or not.

Continue your own education process on the media and participate or start a group that does the same for others in our community. Be aware of how advertising impacts how you spend your money, and on the products you buy for your children, others, and your household. Purchase educational books as presents rather than video games, toys, and non essential clothing.

Part 3
ECONOMICS

"Game recognizes game."

--Popular idiom

IGNORANCE IS REQUIRED
For the System to Work

Capitalism: an economic system based on private ownership of property and business, with the goal of making the greatest possible profit for the owners.
Cambridge Dictionary of American English

Capital: 1. The state of having capital or property; possession of capital. 2. The concentration or massing of capital in the hands of a few; also, the power or influence of large or combined capital.
The Century Dictionary

This is about us, not others. But for comparison purposes:

- 25% of African Americans are below the poverty level, compared to 9% of whites, 25% of Native Americans, 22% of Hispanic Americans and 12% of Asian American *
- 36.7% of black children under 5 years old live below poverty compared to 12.5% of white children *
- 21.5% of black families live below poverty compared to 7.8% of white families *
- In 1900 the accumulated wealth of African Americans constituted less than 1% of America's wealth. In 2005 the accumulated wealth of African Americans constitutes less than 1% of America's total wealth *
- The "official" unemployment rate for blacks as of July 2005 is 9.5%, for whites it is 4.3%, and for Hispanics its 5.5% *
- Roughly 50% of black adults have what would be considered "bad" credit

In the early 1990s, then Speaker of the House Newt Gingrich was invited to speak at the National Black Journalists Convention. When asked what he planned to do to address the problems in economic development by blacks, Newt said, "Black people don't seem to have good business sense…"

Based on earnings, if African Americans were our own nation, we would rank as he 11th wealthiest nation in the world, higher than both North American neighbors Canada and Mexico. We have been in America for close to 400 years, yet recently arrived immigrants and refugees are making more economic advancement than we are. Although we should applaud others for their advancement rather than "hate on them" as we often do, we have to wonder, what is hurting our progress.

*Source: US Department of Labor

59

In the space below, write down some of the reasons why you believe black people have had such a difficult time establishing businesses, being producers of goods rather than simply consumers, and employing our own people.

Here are some of the reasons we suspect:

- Others bring specialized skills from their land of origin, maintaining ties to that homeland, including economic ties, import/export opportunities and financial assistance, often producing specific goods based on the natural resources of that homeland.
- American blacks not only had that cultural history stolen, they were instead developed as a source of labor, trained at providing service to others rather than producing their own goods. This training, along with laws prohibiting land ownership and business development by blacks, caused a psychological dependency for others to provide for us.
- Because of some of the same laws, when blacks did invent and develop goods, machinery, and technology, others confiscated and capitalized on these advancements (refer back to Inventor's List)
- While there once was a thriving black business community in this country, but after segregation ended, we abandoned those businesses in favor of those from which we were previously banned.
- Due to our conditioning by the media, we have allowed ourselves to be programmed into possibly the most materialistic group of people on earth—blind consumers without a base to produce any of what we consume.
- A deep-seated, psychological fear of independence & self-determination.

Of course, there continue to be racially motivated bias and double standards in business loans and trade restrictions, but there are many self-imposed hurdles caused by our apparent lack of understanding of America's economic system, our materialism and consumerism. As we've all heard, "game recognizes game," so if we're truly to become an economic player, we have to understand the rules.

UNDERSTANDING CAPITALISM

While they hold onto their loaves, we can't wait to spend our crumbs. And they laugh at us, 'cuz our crumbs are what their loaves are made of.
--Ise Lyfe, "Will We Ever Get It Right?"

As we know too well, black people in America live disproportionately in poverty. Poverty, like wealth, is based on the economic system in which a person lives. In America, that system is capitalism. Since we live in a capitalist economy, we are forced to play along by the rules of that system—whether we choose to or not. The scary thing is that the majority of Americans (and particularly black people in America), are playing along without taking time to know what those rules are. As a result, we continually put ourselves in a position to weaken our economic standing while strengthening someone else's.

In 1776, the same year the United States declared its independence from England, Adam Smith staked his place as one of the founding fathers of this country when he wrote a book, called *An Inquiry into the Nature and Causes of the Wealth of Nations*, which outlined the foundations of capitalism.

What Smith uncovered is that capitalism is based on property-ownership. But not just any property qualifies. The "capital" in capitalism is *productive property*—in other words, property that can be put to some productive use in exchange for money or other consideration.

In his book, he wrote:

> *The stock that is laid out in a house, if it is to be the dwelling-house of the proprietor, ceases from that moment to serve in the function of a capital, or to afford any revenue to its owner. A dwelling-house, as such, contributes nothing to the revenue of its inhabitant; and though it is, no doubt, extremely useful to him, it is as his clothes and household furniture are useful to him, which, however, makes a part of his expense, and not of his revenue.*

According to this definition, no matter how many cars, diamonds, or chinchilla coats we own, we are worse off economically, because those products don't have any productive value. Chances are if we do choose to sell or trade those items, they will have depreciated in value. Instead of generating real wealth, which may lead to future security for us and our families, we often get caught up in the *appearance* of wealth. That need to appear successful takes money from our pockets and puts it into someone else's.

Write or talk about things you've bought just "for show."

_____

_____

_____

_____

Looking back now, what are some more important things you could have used that money for?

_____

_____

_____

_____

In 1860, 98% of black people in America were slaves, and blacks owned .5% of the national net worth. In 2000, though long-considered free, that number hadn't changed much, we still held less than 1% of the wealth. How could this be, with Oprah, Bill Cosby, and all the millionaire ball players, singers, rappers we keep hearing about? The truth is, those few people have improved their financial well-being, but the rest of us have gotten worse-off trying to look like them. We've borrowed ourselves into financial ruin with overspending, high car-notes, credit card debt and collection agency fees. As the country has gotten richer, we've earned higher salaries and gotten more stuff to show for those salaries, but we've sorely missed the opportunities to put that money into savings accounts, real estate, or business ventures that we can pass along to our children. Instead it's going into the pockets of Cadillac, Wal-Mart, and Nike.

According to Target Market News, a black consumer spending research company, in 2002, the year of the most recent economic crash, blacks spent $22.9 billion on clothes, $3.2 billion on electronics and $11.6 billion on furniture to put into homes that, in many cases, were rented. The Urban League's "State of Black America 2004" found that fewer than 50% of black families owned their homes. A 2003 investor survey conducted by Charles Schwab and Ariel Mutual Funds found that even in homes with equivalent income, blacks saved 20% less for their future or retirement. This type of money management is equal to economic slavery in the current system. You can't spend your way towards the comfortable lifestyle wealth affords. That takes a long history of earning, saving and investing.

The Rich Get Richer

Take a look at these charts showing the distribution of wealth in America. Clearly our spending patterns have helped the rich get richer and have helped the poor (which disproportionately includes us) continue to struggle under the boot of financial oppression. While 5% of the people own over half of the wealth, and the poorest half of the people own less than 3%, we'll still spend our entire paycheck on a platinum chain.

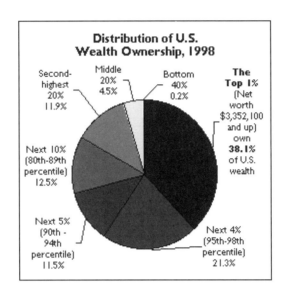

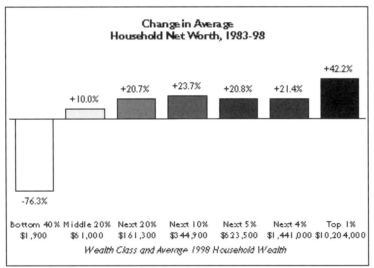

Source: FairEconomy.org

Modern-day capitalism as it's practiced in America has a new and improved, very powerful ally that targets all Americans, but us in particular—the media. Advertising is a multi-billion dollar industry. It uses a host of tools, deceptions and strategies, including:

- Psychology
- Sociology
- Subliminal messaging
- The power of suggestion

- Attaching self-concept and self-esteem to inanimate objects
- Cultural distortion
- Brainwashing
- Exploitation

A key component is to fool us into believing that our identity, self-worth, image, and importance are connected to what we have. Our self-worth is mistakenly tied to the kind of car we drive, the brand of our clothes, what we do for a living, and the amount of money we can flash. As a people, many of us have allowed our cultural self-concept to place importance on the superficial; the meaningless. We prize that which may look good, but has no real value.

The advertising industry tries to convince us that their services are designed, first and foremost, to help us. We need to understand that this is not true. Their only goal is to get our money. Period. They will deceive us into thinking they care about our needs by putting hip hop beats and black faces in their commercials, by telling us how our lives will be enriched by using their products—how we will feel better and be more respected.

This deception by industry works. Except for owning a home or land, most of the items we buy immediately begin losing value the moment we purchase them. Ironically, black people own property at a lower rate than any other group in America. Meanwhile, payday loan/check cashing places replace banks in black neighborhoods, pawn shops flourish, and lottery ticket sales impose an unfair tax upon the poor while teaching them that luck will have more to do with their financial success than hard work.

In order to address our barriers to economic development, we have to understand our own economic habits.

Obtain a tablet or small notebook. For the next week, write down every purchase you make and every bill you pay, no matter how small or insignificant. Write down the day and time that you bought or paid it, where you bought the item from, and its cost.

At the end of the seven days do the following things:

- Add up the totals. How much money did you spend during the seven days?
- How much money did you make during that period of time?
- What percentage of your spending was on necessities (rent, food, electricity, etc.)?
- Of that you spent on food, what was necessity, and what was impulse or junk buying?
- How much money did you put away for savings?
- Are you able to determine what items you bought based on some type of advertising?
- How much money did you spend on cigarettes? Alcohol? Illegal drugs? Partying/nightclubs? Movies/videos/DVDs or other escapes from reality?

What were your general feelings about how you spent your money during the seven days?

_____

_____

_____

_____

_____

Economic class now equals race as a way to divide our society. Did you know that a credit check is a routine requirement to determine whether someone is able to rent an apartment or house? On an increasing basis, credit checks are a part of the employment application process, and bad credit can prevent you from being hired for a job. Your credit rating determines your ability to obtain car insurance and also the rate that you pay. And of course, bad credit will prevent you from home loan approval, and forces many to spend their lives as renters or pushes them into the hands of predatory lenders.

It has gotten to the point where we _must_ educate ourselves on advertising, consumerism, the global economy, capitalism, credit, investments, and most importantly, materialism; and we have to pass those lessons on to our kids. Young people control much of what America spends, and black youth have disproportionate power in defining what youth culture is. Therefore, that handful of companies that are the media giants find it imperative to target young black people into being mindless consumers. As they define "cool" for the rest of the world, the dollars just stack up for the corporations.

Until we stop collectively embarrassing ourselves as black people by our almost complete lack of thinking regarding our finances, others are not supposed to respect us or our spending power. We will continue to serve as the "starter kit" for anyone trying to start a business in America, or anyone looking to exploit others for financial gain.

CAN A BROTHER GET A JOB?

Every man should be able to support himself financially in a legal manner that benefits his community rather than hurting his community. The development of self-reliance, responsibility, and skills should begin early in a boy's life.
--Author Unknown

Recently, there have been a number of articles written nationally and locally on the deteriorating situation of black men in America. These articles are based on studies that have shown that despite a period of prosperity for the country since the mid-1990s, the situation for black men has gotten worse. While the rest of the country has prospered since the mid-to-late 1990s, our situation has gotten worse. *A listing of those articles appears at the end of this section.*

According to these reports, among the biggest hits we have taken seems to be our rising joblessness rate. In this text, we've discussed capitalism, materialism, payday loans, credit and business ownership, but the basic necessity of obtaining a j-o-b seems to be the most pressing concern for our brothers.

Understand the Job Market

For most of the 1900s and before, a man could earn a livable wage with little or no education. There were many jobs that didn't require higher education or advanced technical skills. Steel mills, laborers, farming, trades, small businesses, warehouse, manufacturing and maintenance jobs allowed many black men to purchase homes and support their families. Due to the changing economy, many of these jobs no longer exist; those that do no longer pay a livable wage (a wage high enough to support yourself and your family).

There are a number of factors that make it harder than ever to obtain livable wage jobs. Some of these are:

- Wages have not kept pace with inflation; therefore a dollar made now is not equal to a dollar made 30 years ago.

- Cheaper labor from immigrants and refugees working in low-paying jobs (Before we start the cry of immigration reform, there is no judgment here. These are often jobs that many Americans wouldn't consider taking for themselves, as if we are above hard work).

- The elimination, as stated above, of most "blue collar" (semi-skilled) jobs that pay livable wages. Auto factories, steel production, and other industries have downsized and/or moved their plants from America to other countries at the expense of the workers in both places.

- Exporting (so-called "outsourcing") millions of jobs to other countries where the laws are more lax, labor is cheaper, and companies don't pay for healthcare or retirement benefits, therefore the company's profit is greater.

- Rising costs of college tuition. Financial aid (apart from student loans) is down and costs are up. It is much harder now for a person to wait tables at night to pay their way through college.

- The elimination of many trade schools that trained individuals to obtain livable wage jobs in fields like plumbing, wielding, auto repair, or electrical work.

- Public schools have deteriorated to an all-time low, focusing on flawed standardized tests rather than the child as a whole-learner.

- Specific skills are required to earn a livable wage now. In the technology sector, many new jobs were created as others were lost, yet we haven't kept pace with the learning curve in order to take advantage of this growing industry.

Among the most significant facts that black men need to realize about today's job market is: Business is about one thing—Money. No one is going to *give* you a job. You have to be able to sell yourself to the company. If a company doesn't feel it will benefit by having you as an employee, and that you will fit into their company, they will not hire you. This isn't to tell you to "sell out," but that you have to understand corporate culture if you want to make those high salaries sometimes associated with it.

How We Contribute to Our Own Difficulties in Obtaining Employment:

Lack of knowledge about the job market. Often, we complain about lack of work while we possess little or no understanding of the job market. What types of jobs are available? What skills are required for these jobs? What can you learn about the companies hiring for these jobs?

Simply reading the Sunday Employment sections in the largest newspaper in your area can answer some of these questions. Read the articles and go through the want ads. You will see how many listings there are for various types of employment and what the demand is. It has been said that *finding* a job is the most difficult job there is. For every 10 applications you fill out, you might get one interview. It is a humbling, frustrating task at times, and it ain't easy. It takes a great deal of skill to hunt successfully for a job. The only way to obtain these skills is to put in work (just like in the streets).

How much time have you spent giving serious thought to the type of career you would like?

What have you done to acquire the skills and knowledge to obtain such jobs?

Difficulty filling out a job application. Brothers, part of this comes down to basic writing and reading skills. We need to know how to print or write accurately with proper spelling and grammar. It shouldn't be hard to practice writing the information you will need to put on a job application accurately. Most applications ask for basically the same information. Once you've collected the information you'll need for an application, keep that information (or a copy of the application) in a safe place and bring it with you each time you plan on applying for a job. It will make the process so much easier the next time.

If you need additional assistance, there are a number of organizations specializing in employment workshops, which include help in filling out a job application. These groups can even help those who have difficulty finding a job because of past criminal records. They exist to help, so don't be afraid to ask them or a friend who has a job. Once the first application is done, it gets easier.

> **Do you have ready access to the information you'll need for a job application (dates/addresses of past employment, reference names and telephone numbers, etc.)?**

Difficulty writing cover letters and resumes. This takes even more skill and practice than filling out a job application. Again, employment workshops and job readiness programs provide guidance in this area, or you can do a search on the internet to see how resumes and cover letters are written. Everyone should have a cover letter available, preferably saved on computer (if you have one, or a disk if you don't) so that you can make changes and adjustments according to the job you are applying for.

> **Do you have a resume on paper or on a disk? Do you know how to write one or how to get one written for you? (you should always know how to write you own)**

Having a valid driver's license & clean driving record. Any job that may involve driving will require a driver's license and decent driving record. There are jobs for bus, truck, cab and delivery drivers that we can't even consider applying for because we lack the discipline to get a license before we drive, pay our tickets and drive according to the laws of the land.

> **Do you currently have a valid drivers license? Do you have car insurance? What does your driving record look like?**

Difficulty passing a drug test. Many jobs – including all driving jobs – will require an initial drug test and often periodic drug tests on an ongoing basis. When we sell drugs we put ourselves in a position to be locked up. When we use drugs we put ourselves in a position to be unemployable. Get help if you need to, but cut 'em loose.

The type of hustle required to be successful selling drugs trains you never to be able to hold a job—no set schedule, the instant financial gratification (cash made each night), the late nights, some even pop pills to stay up longer hours. The amount of money made versus the number of hours put in rarely adds up to the money to be made at a legal job.

Do you currently sell drugs? If so, besides the money, why?

Do you currently use drugs of any kind? If so, why do you do so?

Interview/communication skills. The theme of our book is partly the distorted self-concept we hold of ourselves. Part of this is the language we use, and part of it is how we present ourselves. No one is asking you to sell out, just be aware of the image we present. Some of the brothers that are selling you the hard, ghetto persona are the real sellouts, since they are buying into a self-destructive prescription.

It doesn't make you a punk or a sellout to be able to talk and dress in a manner that allows you to function in mainstream society. You don't even have to change who you are at home or with you're friends. Being able to communicate in two worlds is called being bi-lingual. Some call it "code-switching." You have to learn which code is in use at any given time. Historically, black people have been the most adept at this skill, and can continue to be so. Giving up that ability is only hurting us.

We're being played if we think that work is for "suckas," or we're holding onto a narrow idea of what it means to be black. If we take ourselves out of the employable category, who wins?

Have you ever been interviewed for a job? If so, what was the outcome? If not, why not?

Punctuality – getting to work everyday, on time. This is a classic example of how we often take pride in something that works against us. The concept of "CP Time" doesn't work in the work world. When we are able to obtain employment, we often sabotage ourselves by coming late, missing work, and not comprehending why <u>they</u> don't understand our situation.

Some of us live such chaotic lives (late nights, chasing women, drinking, and so on) that we're constantly running late or having crisis in our lives. This doesn't work when trying to hold a job. Make it your personal goal to go to work everyday, on time. Generations ago, black men didn't miss work and didn't arrive late, so don't say punctuality is a "white thing." It is about handling our business.

Do you currently have a job? If so, how long have you had it?

If you are not employed now, why not? Are you currently looking for work? If so, how much time each day do you spend looking? If not, why not?

What were the reasons for leaving, or being let go from jobs in the past?

Getting along with others in the workplace. If you're a brother – young or old – who hasn't worked much in your life, once you obtain a job you have to learn how to deal with co-workers and/or customers. Sometimes these people's reality is going to be so different from yours, it will be hard to see eye to eye. Other times, it may feel like they are disrespecting you. We have to be able to work through those situations. Often, the only emotions black men have allowed ourselves to feel are pain and rage. In the workplace, those emotions will get you fired. Controlling them is easier said than done, but as we train ourselves to feel other emotions, deal with difficult people and situations, we'll be in a better position to get along with others and keep our jobs.

Another key element is to come from a position of strength. In other words, *always* handle your business to the best of your ability. Learn to take pride in your work regardless of what it is. People respect those who respect themselves. At work, self-respect can be shown by doing a good job.

Also, be respectful to all and conduct yourself in a professional manner, even with co-workers. Some of the biggest mistakes some brothers make are messing with the women at work, clowning, or trying to "get over" on the boss. This can be in the form of taking their property, taking too long for breaks, trying to sneak in late, and so on. If you're new to the world of work, it is important to learn from your mistakes. Some brothers go from one job to another, making the same mistakes over and over.

Have you ever been fired from a job? If so, for what reason(s)? If you've been fired from more than one job, were the reasons the same or similar each time?

Have you worked to eliminate the actions that got you fired in the past? If so, what have you done to change the behavior/action? If not, why not?

Having a strong work ethic. Old-school black people used to have a saying: "You have to be twice as good, and work twice as hard to compete against white people." To be honest, many of our people today don't have the work ethic of those who came before us. Part of our distorted self-concept is the slick talking, cool, get-over-with-as-little-effort-as-possible mentality. As a result, many of us really don't know how to work hard. Others don't think it is "cool" to work hard. We have all experienced a person who is rude, lazy, unprofessional and acts as if they are doing you a favor by doing their job.

Working hard and priding oneself on excellence isn't a matter of "bustin yo ass for the man," rather it's a matter of personal pride and integrity. Not only is it important for our people to work hard, but also to be the best at what we do. We need to understand all elements of our jobs and the skills that go along with it. That way, it enables us to move up the corporate ladder, start our own businesses, and teach others. Some of us need to be honest with ourselves and admit that our work ethic isn't what it should be. A shift in attitude can correct this.

Is there a time where you feel you gave maximum effort at something? When was the time and why was it important for you to give such an effort?

Is there a time where you know you <u>didn't</u> make an effort at something? What were the results, and you did you not give your best effort?

Working towards our career objectives. We often appear not to give much thought to how we want to support ourselves financially. Livable wage jobs don't fall from the sky, and no one "owes" us these types of jobs. We have to give some serious thought to what we want to do, then work towards educating ourselves and gaining the skills necessary to do the work. This might mean completing school, obtaining our GED, taking some courses at a community college or enrolling in one of the few trade schools that remain.

Making money illegally trains you <u>not</u> to be able to function in a job. How much time have you spent making money illegally compared to making money in a legal way?

Take a moment to add up how much time do you spend watching TV, playing video games, partying, chasing women, getting high or chillin' with your boys compared to preparing yourself to obtain the type of job/career/business you want?

Have you ever thought about taking a class at a community college or technical school? If you haven't, why haven't you even thought about it? If you have, what has stopped you from doing so?

Allowing ourselves to be psychologically played. It is no accident that we are bombarded with images of black men flashing cash, sporting expensive vehicles with rims, expensive jewelry, clothes and sound systems. If your value system is based on material possessions, the long-term process of working, saving, investing and planning will be a foreign concept to you.

Whether you are a young brother or old, what is your career goal? How did you decide upon this choice?

Is your career goal something which you commonly see black men doing on the media (athlete, performer, etc.)?

If so, are you letting someone else program or brainwash you into being what they want you to be?

Should military service be an option? We understand and greatly respect why past generations of black men served their country in the military. However, the dynamics have changed. When you are a soldier in the military, you become the face of a country's military and foreign policy. Whether or not you fully believe in those policies, you will still be leading their advancement throughout the world. Poor people and black people consistently end up serving on the front lines of wars and other military actions, more likely to shoot and be shot at. Often times, those people doing the shooting on both sides have more in common with each other than those men ordering the shooting (they are brown-skinned, poor, undereducated, and looking for a way out of their poverty).

Black people should do some deep soul searching before deciding military service is the career choice for them. However, this is an individual decision. Before enlisting, don't talk only to recruiters. Visit a VA hospital or homeless shelter and ask veterans how they were treated during their military service and once they came back from serving their country. Look at the current administration and its take on world affairs. Ask yourself where you may be asked to go serve, who you may be asked to shoot, and whether that action fits you're your personal value system. Make your decision with as much information as possible.

There are many different types of jobs, careers and businesses to be had. There are also _millions_ of black men across the country just floating with no direction or purpose. They are engaged in illegal activity, hanging out, or trying to hustle someone else out of theirs. It's as if many of us have given up.

We can keep filling someone else's pockets by filling their jails and prisons. We can keep pimping, stealing from and selling poison to each other. Or, we can rebuild our own communities and rise as a people.

You can do this. Imagine if you spent the same time hustling to obtain a job or grow a business that you do on your illegal hustle. Change would have to come. Our biggest obstacle is in our heads.

A few articles that look at the grim stats:
"Plight Deepens for Black Men, Studies Warn" by Erik Eckholm, New York Times – March 20, 2006

"We Can't Afford to Waste a Resource: Young Black Men" by Jerry Large, Seattle Times – March 26, 2006

"Reports Offer Grim Forecast for Young Black Men" by Michael E. Ross, MSNBC – April 7, 2006

THERE GOES THE NEIGHBORHOOD
Property Ownership & Gentrification

Gen-tri-fi-ca-tion: the immigration of middle-class people into a deteriorating or recently renewed city area; gentrify.
--Webster's Ninth New Collegiate Dictionary

In urban, traditionally black neighborhoods around the country, the practice of gentrification has been taking place. In a general sense, this means the arrival of wealthier (usually whiter) people in an existing urban (often black) neighborhood. This has often led to the displacement of poor people in favor of those with more money as homes are scooped up at bargain prices and renovated or resold.

From a distance, some aspects of gentrification would seem desirable—new investment in the neighborhood infrastructure, increased economic development, and reduced crime. But a closer look shows that most of these benefits are enjoyed by the new arrivals, and long-time residents are once again marginalized.

Once this process begins, the following events may take place:

- As new "investors" move into the neighborhood, many blacks look at these white residents and begin to question what they are doing in "our" neighborhood.

- Remodeling & redevelopment takes place resulting in increased property values and the associated property taxes. Rents increase for those who don't own the properties in which they live.

- Many blacks and other poor people move out to more affordable areas of the city.

- Law enforcement and other services increase. Businesses begin to invest in the neighborhood and many shops and restaurants open that previously would not do business there. Schools may improve.

- The culture of the neighborhood changes, with newer (often white) residents deciding what is desirable, attractive and appropriate. Talk begins about "what a great neighborhood this is becoming." Many begin complaining about various practices they connect with traditional (often black) residents.

- Primarily white "community councils" are formed and the PTA at local schools change and the white residents have a stronger voice in the shape and direction of the neighborhood. Sometimes, these councils look like vigilante groups as they begin to patrol the neighborhoods to take back *their* streets from the so-called thugs, criminals, dope dealers, pimps, undesirables, animals or _____ (fill in your own

75

degrading code word for black males) with the full support of law enforcement and other government resources.

- Within a relatively short period of time, whites begin looking suspiciously at blacks wondering what we are doing in "their" neighborhood.

But before we decry the breakup of the black community, we have to examine whether or not we think a black community is important. Our actions are showing that we may not. Sure, the process of gentrification is again another example of *institutional* racism (though most of us have nothing against the white *individuals* living next door to us), but this is what *we* have done:

Beginning soon after the civil rights movement, those of us who achieved certain professional levels began abandoning our own traditional neighborhoods to move to primarily white suburbs. Our quest to prove we "made it" resulted in removing the professional economic base within black neighborhoods, leaving these neighborhoods poorer, with fewer businesses, lower tax base, and often in a state of neglect. While we were fleeing to the suburbs, many whites—aware of the increasing, urban property values, long commutes and rising gas prices—were passing us in their moving vans to purchase the property we foolishly sold.

Sadly, we as black people often speak of "getting out," or "escaping the ghetto" when we reach a certain income level. Other people work to improve their communities. We remain the main group in America that openly speaks of "escaping" the neighborhoods in which our people live.

While our elders worked to own their homes and create a "black community," many of us in the younger generations don't think about land ownership at all, using our rising income levels to purchase/lease luxury cars, jewelry, rims, sound systems and designer clothes, at the expense of our credit ratings, savings accounts and other investments—including real estate.

This short-sightedness leaves us unreliable to inherit property from our parents and in an ill state to purchase it. Our higher debt and consumer lifestyles makes selling homes for quick cash seem attractive; therefore homes that have been in our family for years may change hands quickly upon the passing of our parents or grandparents. On some occasions, due to drug addiction, gambling problems or high consumer debt, we lost homes to bank foreclosure not long after we inherited them.

We have no plan. When we allow crime, drug dealing, deteriorating conditions, substandard schools and a lack of civic participation in traditional black communities, we are inviting people from the outside to target us for "redevelopment."

Be honest. Have you, or do you know anyone who has lost/sold property in what once was the "black community" due to one of the above reasons?

76

Who was it, what happened, and was anyone in a position to provide financial help or technical assistance?

_____

_____

What can we do?

There are brothers and sisters who know far more than we do regarding economics, investing, property ownership and financial matters. However, every section of this book contains elements of the solution:

- Stop consuming items which begin losing their value as soon as you purchase them (non-essential cars, clothes, jewelry, etc.).
- Stay out of the criminal justice system. Not by trying to "beat the system," but rather by committing illegal acts. We instantly create more single-parent families upon incarceration. It is doubly difficult for a single parent to purchase a home in today's real estate market. You also reduce your chances of getting a home loan.
- Educate yourself. In addition to learning about yourself and your history, discover how economics and credit work, how true wealth is built, and how to save and invest. If you have bad credit, learn how you can improve/repair it.
- Be the stable, reliable person the elders in our families can rely on to help them handle their business—not simply for the selfish purpose of getting what they have—but for the selfless purpose of giving those who came before us the love and care they deserve.
- If you or a family member owns property, KEEP IT whenever possible. Discard our habits of immediate gratification, quick cash windfalls, materialism, and distrust of each other. Help protect our elders from predatory lenders.
- Those who do wish to sell their homes can explore doing so themselves rather than enlisting the services of realtors, or be sure the realtor you choose is working with your best interest in mind—not just the quick sale for him/herself.
- Begin an investment group with the goal of purchasing property together. Learn together the legal ramifications and common pitfalls. Of course, this calls for us to trust each other and to be trustworthy. To do so requires us to discard the psychological slavery we still carry within.

It has been said that wealth in this country is based on property ownership. While many others prepare to pass that wealth on to future generations, we are going to leave the next generation of black Americans in debt. Since we haven't developed the appreciation for property ownership as a valuable investment tool, we complain about someone taking away what we're actually giving away. Yes, gentrification is occurring. If you care about having a black community, let the powerlessness end, and take action to do something about it.

ECONOMICS ACTION STEPS

De-program/re-educate ourselves. Start by doing a comprehensive assessment of our values regarding materialism. Until we understand and are willing to admit to ourselves that we have had our values given to us and been programmed to be thoughtless consumers who judge ourselves and each other based on what we have rather than who we are, all else may not make sense. Perform a simple exercise. Count the number of commercials that are broadcast on a 30 minute television show, then count the number of commercials broadcast in the time between when that show ends, and the next begins. It may help you realize how we constantly are bombarded with the message to "buy, spend, and consume."

Back to Basics. Learn to budget your money and live within that budget. Have some conscious idea of where we spend our disposable income. Are we paying $600.00 per month just to lease a luxury SUV? How about jewelry? Brand name clothes? What are the interest rates we are paying on our credit cards or those items we are buying over time? Open a checking account and savings account. Compare the services each financial institution provides, and their practices regarding investments, charitable donations, training and hiring of people of color, and lending to people of color.

Delayed gratification vs. immediate gratification. In other words, learn patience. As a people, we have been trained to buy those things we want <u>now</u>, whether our budgets can handle it or not. This leads to the payday loan & pawnshop industries, renting furniture, leasing or buying vehicles at ridiculously high interest rates, impulse buying, and materialism as our primary value system. Delayed gratification can be learned, it simply requires patience and discipline. Corporate America and the big media have spent billions of dollars training you to be a mindless, materialistic consumer. It will take some conscious effort on your part to reverse this training.

Make wise credit choices. Pay off your credit cards and destroy them if you have trouble using them wisely. Using credit cards makes it too easy to purchase that which you can't really afford. Everyone should have a general idea of their credit score, and how the financial decisions we make could raise or lower that score. It is your right to receive a copy of your credit report for free once each year (www.annualcreditreport.com or 1–877–322–8228). Monitor your own credit, and work to improve your score each year.

If you own property, keep it. Educate yourself about the various elements of property ownership and be the stable, reliable person that elderly relatives can trust. Be the selfless, rational person who can resolve the petty family disputes when estates are left due to death. Have the family's best interest in mind, not your own short-sighted wants.

Invest in us. Ask yourself and your peers, "What will our neighborhoods and communities be if our best minds live, work, invest and spend elsewhere?"

Part 4
EDUCATION

"You Must Learn."

--KRS-One, Boogie Down Productions

EDUCATION or MISEDUCATION?

When you control a man's thinking you do not have to worry about his actions. You do not have to tell him not to stand here or go yonder. He will find his "proper place" and will stay in it. You do not need to send him to the back door. He will go without being told. In fact, if there is no back door, he will cut one for his special benefit. His education makes it necessary.

--Dr. Carter G. Woodson, *The Mis-Education of the Negro*

A snapshot of the black students experiences in public education is dismal: high dropout rates, low achievement, under-representation in honors classes, over-representation in special education classes, disruptive behavior (often leading to diagnosis of Attention Deficit (Hyperactivity) Disorder (ADD/ADHD) diagnosis, learning disability labels…At times, it seems our educational system does more damage to black males than good.

Reflect back if you can to your own introduction to America's public educational system. If your experience was typical, your experience may have gone something like this:

- You entered school in kindergarten and first grade energetic, enthusiastic and hungry for knowledge, just like the other children, and with comparable skills to those kids.

- Due to different learning and communication styles, cultural differences that led to behavior differences, teachers and other professionals began to wonder about (and possibly diagnose or label you) with a learning or behavior disorder.

- Sometime around fourth grade, you began to lose your enthusiasm, optimism and hunger for learning, and academic disproportionality begins to magnify.

- You started to think about academic success as a foreign concept, a "white thing" that wasn't in line with your self-concept.

- In your early teens, as you were alienated from academic success, you simultaneously became indoctrinated into crime, gangs, drugs and other self-destructive behaviors.

- As a young adult, you often found yourself incarcerated, at times discovering your true self and your untapped potential. For the first time, you may have begun to understand and speak of the self-concepts that led to the deterioration of your life.

The propaganda we are all told is that education is the answer to a better life, and incarceration is the consequence for criminal actions. We would never insinuate that a loss of freedom due to incarceration is a good thing, but why does it so often appear that education results in negative outcomes for black males, while incarceration marks a period of growth and self-discovery for some young brothers? Anyone familiar with prison will not be foolish enough to insinuate that incarceration is a positive and nurturing experience. Rather, this is a catastrophic indictment of our educational system.

It would be unfair and irresponsible to blame America's educational institutions for the demise of so many brothers. True, there have been countless success stories of black men who have successfully navigated that system to go on to great things. Still, it would be equally irresponsible to ignore the connection between traditional education and the deterioration in the quality of life, self-esteem and self-concept of so many of us.

Take a moment to reflect on your own educational history by discussing and writing down your answers to the following questions:

What is your earliest enjoyable memory of school?

What is your first memory of success or pride about something in school?

What do you remember of the first teacher or school professional who helped you feel good about school, education or yourself as a student?

Who was this person and what was their role at your school?

Can you think of a time when school (and its content) was connected to your life or your reality?

When was the period of time—beginning to end—that you felt good about yourself a successful student?

Now write down some thoughts about when that good feeling began to change.

What is your earliest negative memory of school?

Can you remember when you began to be less successful as a student?

Write about the first teacher or other school professional you had a negative encounter with that **was not due** to your own behavior.

Who was this person and what was their role in your school?

When did you change from enjoying school to developing a dislike of school?

Can you remember a specific time you felt the material you were learning did not reflect you or your reality?

Did you ever feel like a teacher or other professional ignored you or didn't expect much from you?

Who was this person and what was their role in your school?

When do you feel your overall attitude towards education changed for the worse?

Now, what was <u>your</u> role in your educational underachievement?

Do you remember a time when you took pride in your school work?

Why was it important to you to do well in school?

Think about it for a moment, and try to remember when this began to change.

Do you remember <u>why</u> it changed on your part? (examples: girls, sports...)

Was there ever a time where you made a conscious choice no longer to try to do well in school?

If you did, why did you make this choice?

As you got older, (middle school/junior high & high school) how much of your time after school hours and on weekends did you spend on schoolwork/homework?

Do you remember a time where you or one of your friends made fun of/ridiculed someone because they did well in school? (Think carefully. Did you ever call anyone a "nerd" or "square" or "geek?")

During your school years, did you ever accuse another black person of "acting white?"

If you did, why did you do so? What were they doing that caused you to feel it was something that white people do, and black people should not?

Where did this belief come from, and is it something you still believe?

Was there a time where you willingly participated in classroom discussions and activities?

Was there a time where you intentionally <u>avoided</u> participating in classroom discussions and activities?

Did what your friends or girls thought about you influence the level of effort you put into school/education/knowledge?

Did you ever notice that many white and Asian students continued to put forth effort in school, while many black boys did not? Why do you think this was?

If you attended school within the last 15 years or so, do you remember any difference between how black students born in America approached academics, and how African immigrants did? What were the differences you noticed?

If you are a young person still attending school, take a serious look at your attitude towards education and how your attitude is expressed by the time and effort you are putting into learning.

If you are an older brother, it isn't too late to look at your own attitudes toward education. This doesn't simply mean school—it can mean knowledge of self, critical thinking, history, current events, or any other food for your brain. What new thing have you learned today?

NEGATIVE from the GET-GO

If you can't remember **ever** feeling as if you were a so-called 'good student' or ever feeling positive about school, don't feel bad. As Jonathan Kozol writes about extensively in his book *Savage Inequalities* there are troubling differences between inner-city schools, the schools primarily attended by black students, and suburban or private schools with a majority of white students. Some of those differences are:

> The most skilled, enthusiastic and experienced teachers are assigned to rural/private (white) schools at higher pay, while inexperienced, poorly trained, mediocre and "problem" teachers generally are assigned to urban (black) schools at lower pay.

> Because of funding formulas, tax revenue bases, fundraising resources and alumni, rural/private schools on average have a budget 2 – 3 times greater than comparable urban schools.

> Rural/private schools routinely have functional buildings, enough books, staff, libraries and computers, while it is common for urban schools to be inadequate in all of these areas.

> Rural/private schools inherently have high expectations for students to internalize, while urban schools promote a sense of low expectations for students to internalize.

> Rural/private schools promote academics while urban schools often promote athletics.

> In most rural/private schools, advance and honors classes are the norm and are in abundance, while such classes tend to be rare or non-existent in urban schools.

> In rural/private schools parents are embraced as partners in the academic success of all students, while urban schools often alienate, blame and distance themselves from parents.

> America's educational system is Eurocentric in nature, leading white students to feel education is a reflection of their way of life, while it often has the opposite impact on black students/communities.

> Educational institutions take credit for successful students while blaming parents for the failures of unsuccessful students. Neither of these beliefs necessarily hold true.

America is a capitalist nation. If we believe that education is the key to getting a good job (and therefore our financial success), then school success for all would mean a level playing field as we attempt to grab our piece of the pie. Those who have fought for the most capital are not going to release all that they've fought for and provide an equitable education system.

The school system was built on the idea of creating a strong proletariat (those without capital, who "sell" their labor to those in ownership—a working class).

In his book, *Principles of Public Education*, written in 1918 and which serves as the model on which our school system was built, Alexander Inglis outlines the functions of compulsory education. As retold by former New York teacher of the year John Taylor Gatto those functions are:

1) The *adjustive or adaptive* function. Schools are to establish fixed habits of reaction to authority. This, of course, precludes critical judgment completely. It also pretty much destroys the idea that useful or interesting material should be taught, because you can't test for reflexive obedience until you know whether you can make kids learn, and do, foolish and boring things.

2) The *integrating* function. This might well be called "the conformity function," because its intention is to make children as alike as possible. People who conform are predictable, and this is of great use to those who wish to harness and manipulate a large labor force.

3) The *diagnostic and directive* function. School is meant to determine each student's proper social role. This is done by logging evidence mathematically and anecdotally on cumulative records. As in "your permanent record." Yes, you do have one.

4) The *differentiating* function. Once their social role has been "diagnosed," children are to be sorted by role and trained only so far as their destination in the social machine merits - and not one step further. So much for making kids their personal best.

5) The *selective* function. This refers not to human choice at all but to Darwin's theory of natural selection as applied to what he called "the favored races." In short, the idea is to help things along by consciously attempting to improve the breeding stock. Schools are meant to tag the unfit - with poor grades, remedial placement, and other punishments - clearly enough that their peers will accept them as inferior and effectively bar them from the reproductive sweepstakes. That's what all those little humiliations from first grade onward were intended to do: wash the dirt down the drain.

6) The *propaedeutic* function. The societal system implied by these rules will require an elite group of caretakers. To that end, a small fraction of the kids will quietly be taught how to manage this continuing project, how to watch over and control a population deliberately dumbed down and declawed in order that government might proceed unchallenged and corporations might never want for obedient labor.

We need to start by redefining education specifically for our people in order to help all of us better understand how the game is played. That includes teaching our kids to think critically, encouraging creativity, and helping them to find the quiet and solitude that facilitates inner dialog (as opposed to filling that time with CDs, video games, cell phone conversations and television). As flawed as the school system may be, they can understand it and navigate it successfully. Expect greatness from them academically, intellectually and socially. Only then will we be able to raise a community of well-educated, thinking men and women.

REDEFINING EDUCATION

Over the years, many strategies have been used to increase academic performance for black students. Among those have been:

- Recruiting more black teachers
- Bussing black students outside their communities
- Proposals for year-around school
- Tutoring programs
- Mentorship programs
- Remedial classes and the "special ed" industry

For the most part, none of these strategies have worked, and the overall quality of education for all children in America has deteriorated. As stated earlier, something very disturbing about our society is the disproportionately high number of brothers who go through our educational system, end up in prison, and then discover a degree of consciousness and self-identity there. We don't recommend voluntarily going to prison, but for too many brothers, it appears our educational system is not working. It had miseducated us, damaging our self-esteem and self-concept. Many black men need to be in prison based on the crimes they committed. However, prison should not be a place where black men discover their sense of self that they lost, or had taken while going through our educational system. There has to be a better way…

For black boys/men specifically, education should start with knowledge of self. Hopefully you see that we need to promote critical and analytical thinking among ourselves. Other men have many of these questions pre-answered, and their values somewhat predetermined because of their long histories. We can't control the choices brothers make, but we can work to make sure that there is a universal concept of black manhood among us that little boys would be proud to emulate.

> **For each of us, that concept would include answers to the following questions, among others. Take a few minutes to think about your answers.**

Who am I? What do I like and dislike, and where did these feelings come from?

How do I feel about myself? What are my strengths, my weaknesses?

When I think of myself as a black boy/man, what does that mean to me?

What do I know about my history, my family's history, the history of black people in America, and African history?

How does this knowledge make me feel? Good? Bad? Don't care? Never think about it?

What are my values? Am I familiar with words like courage, integrity, consciousness, honesty, respect, morals, and compassion? Do I value these character traits?

If not, what character traits are important to me?

Would I describe myself as a follower or a leader? In what ways have I led, and in what instances have I followed?

How do I view the media (TV, movies, sports, music, entertainment)? Do I feel these entities present a positive image of black men, or negative?

What do I believe are the most important qualities for a black man to have?

Do I like to read? What does education mean to me?

I believe some black boys/men gang-bang, glamorize pimping, sell drugs, or engage in other negative activities because…

What is my knowledge of Africa, African history, and early African civilizations?

The more we understand ourselves and our history, the more prepared we are to learn in these educational systems. We will recognize elements of our educational system for what it is: antiquated, often irrelevant, and serving as feeder for big business and corporate America. We will inherently understand how the educational process is used to weed us out, so we will no longer assist this cause by referring to education as a "white thing" and weeding ourselves out.

We will recognize that there is much to gain within that system as well, gleaning from it what is important and relevant. We will understand the universal value of becoming comfortable with numbers; whether its fractions, algebra, geometry, or decimals. We can show each other and teach our children the real-life relevance of this knowledge. We will use the opportunity to hone our communication skills as we practice reading and writing. While our children will be taught his-story we will teach them and understand our own. The comparison will validate our suspicions and stress the importance of understanding self and our own story. We will know those elements crucial to our unique individual and collective needs.

SYSTEM CHANGE

For years, black people who have attained positions of authority in various institutions have said, "It's more effective to fight for change from within the system." When it comes to education, we have failed miserably in this fight. If it were a real fight—in a boxing ring—the referee might have stepped in by now to stop the brutality. Harsh criticism of our people, but it's probably warranted. Look at the facts:

There are black school teachers, administrators and superintendents throughout the nation, in public and private schools, as well as within institutions of higher education; there are black school board members throughout America; the U.S. Secretary of Education during President Bush's first term was Rod Paige, a black man; due to recent opportunities for Charter Schools in various states around the country, we have had the opportunity to educate our own children, something we have accused others of failing to do.

If we had $1.00 for every time black folks have held a conference, summit, training, call-to-action or town meeting regarding the crisis for educating black children, we would have enough funding to build our own schools to rival the best private schools in the country.
We've gone over and over what we need, including multicultural curriculum, better teachers, blacker teachers, historically accurate history courses, higher accountability for schools and teachers.

Think about the psychological beating our children take with all the discussions of discipline problems, poor academic performance, disproportionality in testing, special education placement, and learning disabled diagnosis. In a most cowardly act, we as black men have allowed our children to take the blame while we have failed miserably to do our jobs. Think about that, brothers. It's no wonder our young men are defining their own definition of black manhood. We provide a cowardly, passive, psychologically dependent image for them to aspire to.

We've heard over and over that change starts at home. Along those lines, we won't change our kids' educational experience, until we first change our patterns regarding learning. Below are some suggestions.

EDUCATION ACTION STEPS

BE FATHERS if we have created children. Almost 70% of our children function without our love, support, nurturing, mentoring and protection. If I am an active father, connect with other brothers in order to help them do the same.

READ! We can't say this enough, especially when it comes to education. Be it African or African American history books, science, math problems, English, foreign language – it all starts with reading. For older brothers, the skills required to function

92

in this age of technology are impossible without reading. Hell, even wanna-be rappers need to have the ability to read and write. Reading needs to become one of the high priorities for black men and boys.

Know thy self. For black men, the term education must begin with knowledge of self. Who are we? Where do we come from? What are our strengths, our weaknesses, our talents, skills, and habits? Are we thinkers or do we act instinctively? Are we followers or willing to think independently? What is our definition of courageous black manhood? Do we live up to this definition? Do traits like integrity, compassion, honesty, accountability, responsibility, and honor hold importance to us? In an age-appropriate fashion, these are questions we all need to be familiar with.

Redefine education. For us, education can not be limited to reading, writing and arithmetic. It must be expanded to mean a quest for knowledge – knowledge of self, our people, our history, America's REAL history, financial management, trade/skill development, critical/analytical thinking. Basically, for our people, education must include the ability to think. To see. To look at our society and recognize game, propaganda, brainwashing, and self-knowledge. If we and our children understand what America's educational system is <u>really</u> about, we can beat it at its own game.

Ability to build/construct. As an older, wiser brother once said, "Every man should be able to build something with his hands. Talk is cheap, but when our young people see us construct a physical object, it sends a completely different message— that men construct, produce, manufacture, & repair." We and our children, boys and girls, must get back to developing skills—plumbing, electrical work, auto repair, roofing, framing, welding, and so-forth. It can start early with grass cutting and other chores. We are gradually becoming a people without manual skills and trades.

Life skills. There is no excuse for any black man or boy not to know how to open a checking or savings account, write a check, balance a checkbook, understand the basics of credit, develop a budget and pay bills, manage our time, utilize public transportation, cook, clean, grocery shop, and understand delayed gratification as opposed to the immediate gratification our people are now known for.

Life-long learning. We need to make life-long learning a high priority. If that means taking a course at the community college as adults, learning an additional trade, online or correspondence courses, or musical instruments. Learning and self-growth is a life-long process and we need to value it as such. We also must start early, especially with black boys. Learning a trade, to play a musical instrument, use a computer, or speak a foreign language are valuable tools for children <u>and</u> adults, promote brain development, enhance self-esteem, and broaden our world view and opportunities.

Environmental education/activism. As descendents of Africa, we are the original environmentalists. However, as we've internalized the American value system of conquering or destroying our environment, as black people we may now be the least environmentally conscious people in this land. We litter, break bottles in our neighborhoods for fun, drive the most environmentally damaging vehicles for superficial status, wear furs for the same reason, and consume some of the unhealthiest products in our society. We need to conduct a paradigm shift within ourselves, expose our children to nature, and act as environmental stewards.

Spirituality. We need to re-institute spirituality among ourselves and our children as part of our holistic education/self knowledge. NOT RELIGION, but rather spirituality. We need to understand, and help our children understand that there is something greater than us, and we are morally and spiritually accountable to that being/entity. This is very different from the institution/business of religion as it is practiced in the black community.

Value shift. As black men and boys, we are regularly displayed as craving the most basic, animalistic, and primitive elements of life. Sex, partying, uncontrolled rage, and simplistic, ignorant behavior are often promoted as "being black" or "keepin' it real." We need to conduct a complete shift from this demeaning and damaging self-concept. Education (traditional & holistic), self-knowledge, reading, and social consciousness need to become our highest priorities, and a core element of black manhood.

Each one teach one. As we adopt these new concepts, definitions, and values about education, we need to make sure to share this information with other brothers - especially those who need it the most. Volunteer as a mentor, visit prisons, jails, detention centers, half-way houses, work release programs, and the streets. Conduct a reading group for black boys at your local school or through a church. You may find schools reluctant to allow you to speak to their students about this - all the more reason to do so. With their failure rate with our children, it's all the more important to organize with some other brothers and do so.

School activism. We have to become active in the educational institutions. We need to be a regular presence for our children as well as other children. A black man at a PTSA meeting as a parent is almost as rare as a pork chop at a Mosque. We need to educate ourselves about the mis-education system we were (and our children now are a part of), and make our presence felt within those institutions. Our own miseducation at the hands of these institutions can cripple our ability to think, understand, and intervene within those same systems.

Activity vs. passivity. Empowerment, action, the ability to believe one can bring about change, are all part of learning. Similarly, passivity, complacency, indifference, and powerlessness are also learned behaviors. Our greatest educational challenge may be to re-educate ourselves into believing in ourselves, each other, and our ability to affect change. We have been taught for hundreds of years to be passive, while black women routinely carry the load. It is time for us to face up to this "educational" challenge. DO SOMETHING!! Anything. Don't talk, philosophize, and pontificate. Get involved. Read. Facilitate a group. Take a class. Mentor a young brother with no father. Just do something to break the passivity and lack of action which plagues us as black men.

Part 5
OUR HEALTH

**Physical, Mental & Spiritual Life
(or Death)**

THE SILENT KILLER

Research has shown that doctors rated African-American patients as less intelligent, less educated, more likely to abuse drugs and alcohol and more likely to fail to comply with medical advice.

> --"Closing the Gap 2003: Racial and Ethnic Disparities In Health Care"

Some medical researchers have begun to suspect that such incidents (of racial discrimination) take a physical toll and may play a role in why black people tend to have poorer health than white people.

> --Rob Stein, *The Washington Post*

The realities...

The infant mortality rate for black infants in the US is 13.9 deaths per 1,000 births. For white infants the rate is 7.1 deaths per 1,000 births.

The life expectancy for a black man in the US is 68.8 years. For white men it is 75.1 years, and for black women it is 75.6 years.

Black people contract various forms of cancer at a rate of 642 per 100,000 people, compared to 542 per 100,000 white people.

The rate of lung cancer for blacks is 108 per 100,000, while it is 72 per 100,000 for whites.

Blacks contract colon and rectal cancer at a rate of 69 per 100,000, compared to 59 per 100,000 whites.

Blacks contract prostate cancer at a rate of 251 per 100,000, compared to 167 per 100,000 for whites.

The death rate from HIV/AIDS is 7 times higher for blacks than whites, and the homicide rate for blacks is 6 times higher than it is for whites.

The leading causes of death in America, separated by race:

Blacks
1. Heart disease
2. Malignant neoplasms (cancer)
3. Cerebrovascular disease (a cause of strokes)
4. Diabetes
5. Accidents
6. Homicide
7. HIV/AIDS
8. Respiratory (lung) disease
9. Nephritis syndrome (inflamed kidneys)
10. Septicimia (blood poisoning)

Whites
1. Heart disease
2. Malignant neoplasms
3. Cerebrovascular disease
4. Respiratory disease
5. Accidents
6. Diabetes
7. Influenza & pneumonia
8. Alzheimer's disease
9. Nephritis syndrome
10. Suicide

Frighteningly, 2 of the top 10 killers of blacks are totally preventable—those being HIV/AIDS and Homicide. If we break down the statistics further, the situation becomes even grimmer for black men, since we kill each other in far greater numbers than the sisters do. When black women *do* die from homicide, it is usually a man who takes them out. Similarly, we are normally the ones transmitting HIV to black women.

Do your own count.

> **Think back over your life and write down the various ways black men you've known (family member, relatives, friends, or brothers you knew) have died.**

_____

_____

_____

_____

_____

If your list is anything like ours there are the older brothers who died from heart attacks, cancer, and diabetes. You may also have listed brothers who died from murder, suicide, car accidents, AIDS, and being taken out by police.

Brothers, it's time to get off the belief that real men don't go to the doctor, think about our health, or think about what we put into our bodies. In too many cases, when we don't take care of ourselves physically, mentally, and spiritually, we're hurting or killing others in the process – like women, children, and other innocent bystanders.

The cultural connection to health

As Jawanza Kunjufu said in his book, *Countering the Conspiracy to Destroy Black Boys*, "Culture is everything." It seems that among the intangible benefits of having an ingrained ethnic or cultural heritage is better health and a longer, more productive life.

1. University of Washington scientists conducted the Seattle Kame ("kah-may") Project from 1991 to 2002 on about 2,000 Japanese Americans. Some of the project's findings:
   - Elderly Japanese Americans who had strong ties to their heritage were less likely than others to suffer from dementia or cognitive decline
   - Those who learned Japanese or lived in Japan when they were children were least likely to have mental decline
   - A connection with Japanese culture has a positive impact on life expectancy
   - The Japanese language may play a role in building up more nerve connections in the brain

   Source: NikkeiConcerns.org / Seattle Times

2. After the holocaust in World War II-era Europe, Jews were able to battle back from the tragedies they had suffered, due largely to the strength they could draw as a unified people. Throughout the war they were able to hold onto a sense of who they were, and one generation later, they were able to prosper culturally and economically as a result of that strength.

3. In 1967, 400 black people left America to reunite with the land they considered their true home. Believing they are the true Hebrew Israelites spoken of in history and the bible, they settled in Southern Israel, and embraced the culture and lifestyle of their ancestors. Only 30 years later, despite family histories in America that included about 30% obesity and similar numbers for high blood pressure, only 5-6% of the African Hebrew Israelites suffer from these conditions.

   Source: Janet McConnaughey, The Associated Press
   Reprinted, kingdomofyah.com

Eating Ourselves to Death?

Among the intangibles like those above, your culture dictates many of the foods we eat. Chinese, Jews, Italians, Norwegians, Irish, Ethiopians, and Kenyans have specific foods which have been a part of their diets for thousands of years. As black Americans, we claim "soul food" as our ethnic food. Many of these foods--Hog's heads, chittlins, pigs' feet, and many of the others—were GARBAGE!

Yes, we made the best out of a bad situation, but let us not be so desperate to create a culture for ourselves that we willingly claim the garbage of our enslavers as some type of delicacy. Our ancestors had little choice but to eat the intestines of pigs. Many of the deep-fried, cholesterol-filled, fat-heavy foods we eat cause obesity and along with the excess weight contribute to high blood pressure, diabetes, various forms of cancer, and kidney failure.

What are your favorite foods and drinks?

_____

_____

_____

If you're like most of our people, there were probably a lot of fried foods, fast food, sugar, salt, soft drinks, and other processed foods that target blacks more than anyone else. Think about the advertisement for these products—Michael Jordan pimping McDonald's, KFC and Pizza Hut sporting black faces and hip hop beats, Lebron James and the puppet with the afro slinging Sprite. The list goes on and on.

While others are breaking free from fast food due to child obesity and diabetes, the corporate pimps continue flattering us into eating food that's so unhealthy, we think nothing of it, even though there are more obese black children and adults than any other group of people. Why is it so easy for others to play us?

Some good news...

According to the CDC, only 6.6% of black people consume alcohol excessively, compared to 10.5% of whites.

While 25.5% of white high school students smoke cigarettes, only 14.3 percent of black students do so.

The good news might stop there, however, in another case of youth having more sense than adults. While 24.3% of while, adult males smoke, 25.5% of black men light up. This is important since those cigarettes that rate highest in tar, nicotine, and other deadly carcinogens have targeted blacks for years (these being the menthol brands like Kool, Newport, etc.), and have often targeted us through our own magazines (Ebony, Jet, Essence).

Now what?

While the lack of knowledge of foods from our land of origin is responsible for some of our habits, what else keeps us eating ourselves to death? Is it because we have become a people trained towards immediate gratification? Are we becoming an increasingly non-thinking, media-driven race? You rarely see obese Africans (and it isn't because all Africans are starving, as the media might have you believe), yet, while there are many restaurants by African immigrants who don't have the same health issues as blacks, we don't adopt their eating habits or eat at their establishments. In fact, it isn't that uncommon to hear us joke and laugh at the foods they eat.

Chemical poison

Let's put the question out: What drugs or forms of alcoholic beverage do you partake in?

_____

_____

_____

What are your reasons for ingesting those things?

_____

_____

_____

One definition of addiction is the willingness to continue use of a specific substance, even though the results of such use have a negative impact on our lives. Also, remember the word **denial.** Denial is a person's inability or unwillingness to see what is obvious to others.

What are the positive results you receive by putting these substances in your body?

What are the negative results?

_____   _____

_____   _____

_____   _____

_____   _____

We are not passing judgment on an occasional beer or glass of wine. We also don't intend to convince anyone that they might be an alcoholic or drug addict. Those are questions you'll have to answer for yourself. However, if your sitting in a jail, detention, or prison cell reading this, or have been charged with drug dealing, it might be time to look at the impact your own behavior is having on you – and our people.

Also keep in mind that substances such as drugs and alcohol have been used to maintain social and political control in America throughout its history. Whether we're talking about alcohol and Native Americans, heroin, crack cocaine and malt liquor in black neighborhoods, your generation of black men wouldn't be the first to be played in this fashion. And you wouldn't be the first to be bamboozled into assisting in the destruction of yourself and your people in this way, either.

Who is *really* getting played here?

OUR PHYSICAL SELVES

This might go without saying to many of us, but we need to start with basic hygiene. We all remember some brother (maybe ourselves) who was known for his bad breath, rotting teeth, or strong body odor. Poor hygiene can have long lasting health, social, and self-esteem problems. While poverty can make it a little more difficult to maintain good hygiene, it is mainly our own personal habits and what we were taught when we were young that sets the standard.

How many of us:

- Brush our teeth at least twice per day & floss regularly
- Bathe or shower daily and after physical activity
- Use deodorant
- Wash our hands regularly, keeping our nails trimmed and clean
- Wash our clothes regularly
- Keep our living quarters clean

We're all familiar with the brother (again, maybe ourselves) who plays basketball for hours, puts his clothes back on, at best, might try to mask the funk with cologne or deodorant, and wears the same funky clothes for days after. To a certain degree we accept poor hygiene more readily than other men do. Maybe our distorted sense of manhood causes us to believe that taking care of our hygiene is somewhat feminine. Maybe our internalized hatred causes a low self-esteem that tells us we're not worth the trouble. In any case, these assumptions ARE WRONG. There ain't nothing manly about being funky, having bad breath, dirty underwear, or rotten teeth. Keeping ourselves neat and clean can be an important first step to boosting a low self-concept. If you don't think it's a problem, ask a sister how many less-than-clean brothers she has been with or who have attempted to get with her.

Just as women teach their daughters about their periods, how to keep their genitals clean, fix their hair, wear makeup and so forth, brothers should do the same with our boys. Of course in too many cases, fathers are not around. But when we are there as fathers, we must be better about having our stuff together, and making good hygiene the standard for black men and boys.

Maintaining our physical fitness

What do you do to keep your body in shape?

_____

_____

We've already discussed some of the things we put into our bodies. Also, with the old stereotype of black men and boys being naturally gifted athletes, this is an area some of us believe will take care of itself. There are also certain sports that we embrace culturally, while we disregard others. These activities tend to be higher profile activities that make us prone to injuries in the long run, or we play them in such a highly-competitive way that we can't fully enjoy the social benefits of group sports activities. While these are great games that offer us so much in the way of physical exercise and skills-building, we need not dismiss certain types of physical activity because of a distorted cultural concept, or because, "brothers don't do that."

Some of the healthiest, yet, overlooked activities by us as black men are:

- Yoga
- Meditation
- Martial arts
- Swimming
- Walking
- Hiking
- Jogging
- Aerobics
- Skiing
- Skating
- Rock climbing
- …and many others

Similarly, we often ignore some other aspects of good physical health, such as maintaining a balanced diet, receiving adequate sleep, and keeping sound mental health.

MENTAL HEALTH

Despite what you might think, taking care of your mental health "ain't a white thing." Due to the stigmas we attach to counseling, therapy and other forms of mental health treatment, many of us are suffering needlessly from a variety of problems. How does our mental health hit us? Some problems are:

- Depression
- Stress
- Rage/anger
- Homicide
- Suicide (including suicide by cop/rival gangs/or a generally suicidal lifestyle)
- Various forms of mental illness
- PTSD - Post Traumatic Stress Disorder (as well as a newly recognized, uniquely black version, Post Traumatic Slave Disorder)
- Anxiety
- Alcoholism and drug addiction
- Sexual promiscuity/STDs/HIV/AIDS
- Domestic violence
- Verbal/physical/emotional/psychological abuse & neglect
- Complacency and stagnation
- Homelessness
- Chronic unemployment/under employment
- Legal/criminal justice problems
- Educational failures

These are but a few of the ways we can be impacted by poor mental health, or not paying enough attention to our mental state. As black men, if we aren't careful to come from a position of strength and awareness we can be especially vulnerable due to the cultural loss we identified earlier. Remember, cultural heritage provides grounding, strength, and mental stability. Our cultural heritage was taken from us and we have allowed a distortion of our self-concept. This distortion causes trauma, chaos, dependence, low self-esteem and self-hatred. It also positions black men as scapegoats for many of American society's ills.

As black men and boys we are over-represented in those areas which can cause stress/mental struggles (poverty, criminal/legal issues, unemployment among them). The racial dynamics in this country and the choices we make because of them lead black men and boys towards a generally more-stressful lifestyle. This has a direct connection to our well-being.

Stress: One of Our Greatest Killers

Each time we experience a stressful situation, there is a chemical reaction in our bodies. We feel it in the form of anger, rage, fear, excitement, or other emotion or reaction that puts us in battle mode. Studies have shown that this rise in adrenaline produced directly contributes to hypertension and heart disease—so-called stress-related diseases—as well as damaging our immune system in ways that make us more susceptible to other illnesses.

Black men tend to feel stress in a variety of ways. Higher unemployment, poverty, racial slights (real or perceived) all contribute to increased stress levels. Therefore some may say that stress is **the greatest single threat to our health.** We don't often talk about it because again, we have the perception that real men don't complain, we just handle our business. Yet, the stress and disrespect we feel from one negative encounter not only has serious physical consequences on our bodies, we react to this disrespect in other instances. We may take it out on our wives/girlfriends, children, or another person who just happens to get in our way after one of these encounters.

Do you recognize stress when it occurs in your life? What are some examples?

_____

_____

_____

There are certain types of stress that are so constant, so ingrained in our daily living, that we don't recognize them as stress, we simply see it as life that is normal for us. Examples such as:

- Being poor. The daily stress of trying to pay bills, eat, maintain housing, and support one's family economically
- Unemployment or under-employment
- Living in an unsafe, stressful, or high-crime area
- Being in some type of relationship where there is regular conflict
- Engaging in illegal activity
- Regularly driving with a suspended license, warrants, or without car insurance
- Having committed some act which causes someone to be looking for you (police, rival gang, someone you have wronged)
- Being the type of person who notices injustices in our society/world
- Dysfunctional family relationships

These aren't just stressful instances, having any of these issues means living a stressful life. This type of stress is one of the main reasons for black men's increased incidence of various diseases.

Read those examples just listed as constant forms of a stressful life style.
Which ones are present in your life?

_____

_____

_____

List those actions or activities you regularly engage in to deal with your stress.

_____

_____

_____

If you had a hard time answering these questions it may be because stress is such a constant in your life, you don't recognize it. Due to poverty, incarceration, racism and lifestyle choices, it's fair to say that no one leads as stressful a life as we do. Such a lifestyle is killing us in the form of various cancers, heart disease, high blood pressure, drugs, alcohol, violence, diabetes, kidney failure, suicide, and homicide. Many of us turn to drugs or alcohol to help us cut through the stress, but these types of escapes are temporary, and tend to lead us towards consequences that increase our stress levels in the end. Those consequences could be financial or legal problems, problems at school or work, or strained family relationships.

Some of the causes of our stress permeate our society. We can't snap our fingers and eliminate poverty, racial bias, unemployment, high crime rates, and so forth. But what we can do is:

1. Recognize stress within ourselves as well as its causes in our environment.
2. Don't hold your feelings inside. They'll come out one way or another, often with hazardous consequences. Develop relationships with other brothers where it is safe to share your feelings, frustrations, and obstacles.
3. Pray. It isn't weak to pray, there are circumstances in life that are greater than we are. It can be comforting to believe there is someone or something in life that we can depend upon that is also greater than we are.
4. Meditate. Like prayer, it can develop peace, tranquility, and serenity.
5. Exercise. Physical exercise counters the effects of stress, helps release toxins from the body, strengthens the immune system, and promotes physical health.
6. Listen to or play music.
7. Read.
8. Be aware of the type of life you lead. How much of your stress are you bringing upon yourself due to the choices you make and life you choose to lead?
9. Refer to the "Core Elements of Black Manhood" list at the end of this book. Being a lying, scandalous individual creates stress. Building upon the character traits on the list can reduce it.

As a people, we expend great deals of energy talking about what someone else is doing *to* us, or isn't doing *for* us. It is time for us to take these simple steps to take better care of *ourselves*.

HOW WE THINK (or Don't)

As black men and boys we have allowed ourselves to be dumbed-down in some respects. If you examine the entertainment being fed to us through music, television and movies, it is clear that we are being programmed to allow our most basic, animalistic impulses to drive our actions. This manifests itself in a variety of ways:

- Our tendency to "go off" or "lose it." We have become known for violent eruptions, and have become linked to confrontation.
- Our tendency to be driven by sexual urges. This is perpetuated through the media. We don't think, don't reason, we just want to be sexual.
- Our growing habit of communicating in a basic, thoughtless manner. Talking loud, cussing in public, or saying inappropriate things without considering their impact.
- The "mob" or "wilding" mentality that can erupt when a large number of black people get together (at parties, nightclubs, concerts, or elsewhere). This isn't the rioting of the 60s based on a specific cause; it is embracing destruction and ignorance for the sake of giving into our most primitive instincts.

Are we increasingly becoming a non-thinking people?

YOUR THREE BRAINS

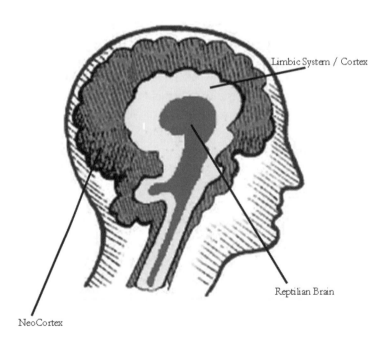

Take a look at the diagram of your brain above.

108

The reptilian or core of the brain is the section responsible for our fight/flight responses and sexual urges, among other things. The actions that develop in this part of our brain are largely reactions to external circumstances or biological urges. There is no processing here. We just act. You don't need to think about whether you are hungry—your body tells you. You don't have to wonder when you need to use the bathroom—it is instinctive. The core of your brain is also the smallest portion of our brain, the one we share with all animals, from snakes and lizards on up. When we act from this place, it is an action any animal also can do. Pause to think about that the next time your pulse jumps and you instinctively buck up against someone for mean mugging you at the bus stop.

More complex processes happen as thought moves to the cortex and neocortex. Emotions are processed, critical thinking happens and we develop the higher thought that separates us from beasts. Only when all three sections of our brain are at work are we truly living our potential. When we do, we are able to identify more of our emotions than pain or rage. We can understand fear, frustration, disappointment and a host of other feelings that may be at work, and we are able to think critically about where those feelings may stem from. We are also able to examine possible consequences for our actions in split-second instances of anger, and choose the most appropriate behavior for the situation at hand.

From which part of your brain do you act?

Think about the last time you "went off" on someone (verbally or physically). Before the anger or rage erupted, what other emotions led up to the confrontation?

What were the outcomes or consequences of the rage?

Thinking back, what other possible reactions could you have taken to the situation?

RELIGION and SPIRITUALITY

Black Churches continue to promote themselves as the preeminent institution within the black community. While we don't want to spend time attacking religious institutions, the current deterioration in our communities and the decreasing impact of black churches on our communities nationwide requires us to consider carefully the type of churches to which we belong. Although some heads of these churches might say otherwise, our churches and those who run them should be held as accountable as any other institution, if not moreso.

The history of the Black Church

- Often initiated social & political movements (segregation, Jim Crow, Viet Nam war, slavery, civil rights) resulting in positive social change
- Lead in the civil rights movement
- Served as the unofficial "social service" agency of the black community
- Was relevant to the current issues that took place in the black community
- Were neighborhood institutions where local people gathered for various purposes
- Church members knew those in the community, and those in the community knew a number of church members
- Had a strong black male presence among its membership
- Had a strong youth presence among its membership
- Someone in the family was connected to the church, therefore all members of the family were influenced by it
- Was based more on action than flamboyant doctrine
- Few "televangelists," fewer mega-churches, less money flowing through churches & fewer churches in black communities

The Black Church today

- Is often rampant with scandals of sexual misconduct by the head of the church
- Have increased in numbers dramatically
- Has less attendance by black men
- Has less attendance by youth
- Has been replaced in service to the community by ineffective government-funded programs
- Often has no connection with its surrounding community
- Is often out of touch with the most immediate and crucial issues in the black community
- Has been negatively impacted by the "Black Leadership Syndrome"
- Is often used by men (and some women) of questionable integrity as a means to obtain power and influence
- Is often ineffective due to church leaders aligned with politicians to maintain social control of the masses of black people

110

- Sometimes led by individuals who are almost pimp-like in their behavior & materialism
- Is dominated by televangelists who are dishonest, manipulative & willing to exploit the sick, marginalized, and desperate for their own financial gain
- Sometimes practices extreme materialism
- Often practices elitism
- Becomes an addiction to some without the internal spirituality the doctrine speaks to
- Almost *never* work together across denominational boundaries to pool resources or work together on issues impacting black people

We know, we know. This will create a great outcry among many in the Black Church. Yet, there are others who readily admit privately that these dynamics often dominate some black churches.

What is your experience with church?

As far as you can remember, when did you first begin going to church, how often did you attend, and do you still go?

_____

_____

_____

If you do not attend church, why don't you? Or, if you continue to attend church, why do you do so?

_____

_____

_____

If you do attend church:

Does your church have a Men's Group?
Does it have a Youth Group?
Does the Youth Group teach the youth about black history?
Do the images of Jesus, angels and other divine figures look like you, or are they depictions of white people?
Does your church conduct street outreach to young men at night?
Does your church conduct various groups throughout the week such as AA (Alcoholics Anonymous), NA (Narcotics Anonymous), Domestic Violence victims and/or batterers, or other such groups with participation by volunteers of the church?
Do members of your church regularly go to youth detention facilities, local jails or prisons to provide spiritual assistance for male and female inmates?

Can your church provide any level of temporary shelter to **one** homeless family in need? Or rather, *would* your church do so?

Does your church provide any level of service to those seeking employment, housing, financial assistance, legal advocacy or counseling?

Does your church do any level of community organizing?

Does your church pool its financial resources with other churches across denominational lines to provide housing, educational assistance, or economic development?

Is the Minister/Pastor/Bishop/Reverend of your church easily approachable to anyone in the church regardless of status?

Does the leader of your church empower others to be leaders in certain areas?

If you attend church and answered the questions, what it your general feeling about your church and what it does for black people?

_____

_____

_____

We are not suggesting to anyone that they attend *or* distance themselves from church. Viewing BET on Sunday and any early morning will clearly show how some black religious institutions have gone to the extreme in exploiting our people. Necessary ingredients for such exploitation are hopelessness, desperation, and the need to look beyond ourselves for solutions. While that is one of many things our Higher Power does for us, it can be risky to lay such hope with a man (or woman) who says they represent God/Allah.   We should hold them accountable for their actions and the policies of the church they lead. Each of us, then, can make up our own mind as to whether the church, mosque or synagogue we attend really is helping others or not.

HEALTH AND SPIRITUALITY ACTION STEPS

- **Visit a health professional.** Whether it means going to a doctor or visiting a free or reduced cost health clinic, visit a doctor. Your blood pressure, cholesterol levels and general physical health are extremely important to know. Also, review health issues that run in your family such as diabetes, heart disease, high blood pressure and various forms of cancer. Again, many of us pay more attention to how our cars or sound systems operate than we do our own bodies.

- **Get tested for HIV.** It can be scary, but get tested. HIV/AIDS is literally killing our people, and we as black men are the primary reason that black women and, subsequently, black children are contracting the disease. It is better to know, for people are living long, healthy lives with HIV. Once our status is known, we must then live responsible lifestyles & stop operating from the core/reptilian part of our brains. We need to exercise self-control and discipline by practicing safe sex.

- **Eat healthier.** Changing ones diet can be tough. But as black men it is something we rarely think about until health problems force us to. Make a list of everything you eat and drink for one week. At the end of the week, review what you find. Are there those things that are not healthy that you can eliminate? Are there healthy foods that you can begin eating? Learn about the positive effects of eating fruit and vegetables, and the negative impact of fast food, too much red meat, sugar, salt and processed foods.

- **Stop smoking.** I once saw a poster that showed the Grim Reaper handing a cigarette to a little black boy in a tobacco field. Under the picture it said, "They used to force us to pick it, now they fool us into smoking it." As you can see, a common theme that keeps coming up is that of discipline. To stop smoking requires it as does eating healthier and showing a level of self-control around sex.

- **Exercise.** Walk daily. Use the steps. Swim. Meditate. Take Yoga or martial arts. Ride a bike. Just find some way to be physically active. We won't use a great deal of space here because you know you need to do it.

- **Be aware of & reduce stress.** Many of us view our lifestyles as normal. It has always been this way and we have grown immune to it. Do a stress inventory. What are the things in your life that cause you to worry the most? Are these issues within or beyond your control? Do you exercise, meditate, pray, or talk to anyone about it? Or do you stuff it, smoke, drink, over eat or go off on people when your stress level gets high? Answer these questions for yourself. You know what to do.

- **Talk to other black men.** Whether it is part of a support group, recovery group, or just with friends, work on changing the way we as black men support each other. We all—to greater or lesser degrees—go through a variety of experiences that create stress, but we deal with it in isolation. Part of redefining black manhood for us must be to realize there is no shame in sharing our experiences, feelings and problems. We must create our own support structure. We must also find forums where we can share our stories.

- **Be mindful of our mental health.** We need to pay attention to our own mental health. Do we feel hopeless, suicidal, homicidal, lethargic (tired), agitated, restless or full of rage? Do we hear voices? Seriously. There are many different forms of mental illness, and the thing is, most people who are mentally ill or are suffering from some sort of problem, don't realize it. There may be solutions to those mental problems we have, at the same time, maybe it isn't a mental problem, just life. While America is quick to diagnose and prescribe medication, we need to be careful of this. We can look at diet, exercise, rest, meditation, yoga, acupuncture, massage, and naturopathic and homeopathic treatments to explore.

- **Spirituality.** There is nothing wrong with the strong belief in something greater than we are. Figuring out what that means for you is a journey each person should make. For some, religion will make sense for you. For others, another path of meditation or prayer can help you remain centered and connected. You have the ability to think, to act, to make decisions and to analyze situations. Using those skills to understand what you believe is a powerful and important task.

- **Church.** What is the church I attend about? Is the Pastor/Reverend/Minister/Preacher arrogant? What kind of lifestyle does he/she live? Is that wealth at the expense of the membership? Are there allegations of sexual impropriety? What type of community interaction does the church have? Is the philosophy of the church for every member to become a more humane person, or to pass judgment on others? How would the people of the church treat a homeless person who came to worship? How would the church treat a sexual minority? These are questions we need to ask and address in order for churches to return to the type of institutions they still claim to be.

Part 6
FAMILY AND FATHERHOOD

"...we pledge to bind ourselves again to one another;
to embrace our lowliest,
to keep company with our loneliest,
to educate our illiterate,
to feed our starving,
to clothe our ragged,
to do all good things,
knowing that we are more than keepers of our brothers and sisters.
We are our brothers and sisters."

--from "The Black Family Pledge,"
Maya Angelou

ON BEING A FATHER

I cannot think of any need in childhood as strong as the need for a father's protection.
  --Sigmund Freud, father of modern psychology.

No love for my daddy, 'cause the coward wasn't there.
  --Tupac Shakur, "Dear Mama"

The ultimate failure

Nearly 40% of American children grow up in a household without their fathers...

...among African American children, 70% grow up in households without their fathers.

We can't instantly create our own schools to educate us. We can't instantly create livable wage jobs. We can't instantly remove violence from our neighborhoods.

But we *can* instantly and immediately be fathers to our children. It doesn't mean we'll instantly do it well, for being a real father takes time, practice, skill, and role modeling. But that can't stop us from trying, because our children only know of their hunger for a father. They don't care how much money we make, what model of car we drive, the kind of clothes or jewelry we wear, only that we're there to love and protect them.

Our greatest failure as black men may be our failure as fathers to our children.

What role does (or should) a father provide for his children?

- Model the proper way a man lives his life
- Protect children as much as possible from physical, emotional, and psychological harm
- Love them, nurture them, and enhance their self-esteem
- Provide for them financially
- Develop a work ethic
- Showing them how to lead and follow (and knowing when each is appropriate)
- Develop a spiritual understanding or relationship with a higher power
- Emulate appropriate interpersonal relationships and how to treat women
- Help children learn how to think critically and analytically
- Help them feel comfortable protecting themselves physically (when necessary) and avoiding conflict (when appropriate)
- Develop independence & self-sufficiency
- Learning courage, humility, integrity & compassion
- Learn to appreciate art, music and explore their own creativity

- Teach them how to drive and repair a car
- Help kids learn to ride a bicycle, play sports, dance
- Learning how to read and to enjoy it
- Build and repair things around the house
- Protect the community
- …the list goes on and on

Mothers can, and usually do, provide these same lessons. The point is, as fathers we have the potential to give significantly to our children. Like the quote by George Herbert goes, "One father is a hundred school masters." Instead of providing those lessons, we allow the majority of our children to learn them alone, from their mothers, on the street, from TV, or not at all. In fact, **fatherlessness among black children is so common; it has become the norm, rather than the exception.**

For those of us who had fathers back in the day, fatherhood was defined differently than it is now. Fathers were silent enforcers. Disciplinarians. Providers who often worked one, two, or three jobs to provide for their families. You didn't talk to them, and hoped they didn't talk to you, because if they did, a whoopin' might soon follow. They toiled from sunup to sundown. They internalized the stress of being the primary providers.

They went to war, came home, got married, had children, bought a home & car, worked at a job until they retired, often without much more than a sixth grade education. They often drank heavily on the weekend but rarely missed work. They lived a life of second-class citizenship, having to absorb blatant acts of racism unlike anything we've experienced, yet they kept going, taking care of their business. They often built their own homes, fixed their own cars, helped each other, and stood sentry over all of us little knuckleheads in the neighborhood.

These old school fathers catch a lot of flack now. They often didn't hug, kiss, or express affection to their children, didn't change diapers, didn't cook, clean, go to school functions, and were sometimes abusive to our mothers (although not with the regularity **we** are) …

And with all of their shortcomings, they were far better fathers than most of us modern day brothers come close to being.

Many of today's black fathers

- Are absent. 7 out of 10 of our children grow up without seeing that a father is a normal part of the family unit. For many children, this can damage their own self-esteem, because they sometimes blame themselves for our lack of desire to be a constant part of their lives.
- Create "father-hunger" for many of our daughters, who often spend years looking for a man to nurture them the way their fathers should have.
- In relationships where abuse is the norm, we cause many of our daughters to seek the same type of abusive relationships they saw their mothers live through with us, and model abusiveness for our sons to emulate.
- Condemn a third of black children to poverty because of a lack of financial support from us.

- Role-model criminal behavior as a part of black manhood, to the ridiculous extreme that there are sons, fathers, and grandfathers serving time within the same jails and prison walls.

Self analysis:

If you are a young brother (21 & below), do you live with your father?

_____

Have you ever lived in the same household as your father?

_____

If so, what was it like? Did you speak to each other? Did he teach you things? Was he involved in certain aspects of your life (school, sports, areas of interest)?

_____

_____

How did he discipline you? Did he yell at you? Cuss at you? Did he use physical force to punish you?

_____

_____

If he did not do those things, what did he do for discipline?

_____

_____

How did he treat your mother? Was there ever physical violence between them or between your father and any other woman? Was there verbal abusiveness? Was he ever involved with more than one woman to your knowledge?

_____

_____

If you did not grow up in the same home as your father, how often did you see him?

_____

Even though your father wasn't in the same home as you, what are your answers to the questions asked above?

_____

_____

_____

_____

After honest reflection, what <u>positive</u> qualities, traits or behaviors do you feel you inherited from your father?

_____

_____

_____

After the same honest reflection, what <u>negative</u> qualities, traits and behaviors do you feel you inherited from your dad?

_____

_____

_____

Now, if you have kids, how would your children have answered those questions?

_____

_____

_____

_____

_____

_____

_____

Without our direct involvement in their lives, our children are at higher risk for a whole list of negative issues. These include academic under-performance, dropping out of school, drug and alcohol abuse, teen pregnancy, crime, incarceration, suicide, dysfunctional and abusive relationships, cigarette smoking, and having emotional and behavioral problems.

While children in single-parent household are said to be at a distinct disadvantage statistically compared to those from intact families, we can make up for much of that disadvantage by being loving, caring fathers to our children.

Our history as fathers

In most cultures throughout the world, men are defined by their ability to provide for, teach, and protect their children and families. As we know by now, our history is unique in that:

- We were stolen from our land and tribe of origin. The priorities, traditions, customs and strategies we utilized as fathers immediately began to deteriorate once we were taken from our homes. We lost our "home field advantage" as we were taken on strange ships to a foreign land. Immediately upon being loaded onto slave ships, our ability to protect our children, families, and act as men was disallowed. To try to do so often resulted in torture or death, in part as an example to other slaves.

- During 246 years of "official" slavery, and many years afterwards, we were programmed **not** to be men, **not** to be fathers and **not** to protect our families. Again, to attempt to do so was punishable by torture or death. In order to survive, our paternal (fatherly) instincts underwent severe trauma. Imagine being faced with the choice of allowing mistreatment, rape, enslavement and selling of our wives and children in exchange of remaining alive to offer *some* level of protection and guidance. Systemically, fatherhood became *less* of a priority for black men. It had to. We *had* to, over time, minimize those elements of manhood we were prohibited from exercising, and developing alternative methods of exercising our manhood.

- Historically, black men have posed the greatest threat to white supremacy. Therefore, there have been constant attacks to the manhood of black men. Every avenue—cultural theft,

121

brainwashing, torture, lynching, psychological attacks—were used constantly throughout our history. We have yet to recover from this trauma. We were routinely forced to be subservient, docile, and submissive toward white people in front of our women and children. *Imagine what that must have felt like.*

- Other elements of exercising freedom and manhood--education, land & business ownership, accumulation of wealth—were also prohibited. For the majority of our history in America we were "property" with no legal protection or rights. In fact, we weren't considered human.

Imagine - if you can - what it was like

Imagine the degrading experiences our male ancestors underwent. We have never undergone psychological recovery from this trauma, and it continues to manifest itself among us in many ways. Specific to fatherhood, there were undoubtedly countless instances where a black child was exposed to some indignity and looked to their father for intervention, protection or comfort. Or, maybe they learned NOT to look to their father because to do so meant forcing dad to make a choice between ignoring their hurt, or risking his life to intervene.

Imagine the powerlessness, rage and frustration countless fathers faced. What would a father do when he heard that his 13 year old son was being sold to another plantation, likely to never be seen by the family again? Or, learning that his 15 year old daughter had been brutally raped by a friend or relative of his owner?

Maybe it was essential for brothers to psychologically distance themselves from fatherhood or face being driven mad with rage and losing their lives. Not that brothers would not and did not give their lives for their children, but what a choice to constantly be forced to make. Although this might explain part of the reason fatherhood has become less important to far too many black men over the generations, those conditions no longer exist.

Today, we have black men going out of their way to avoid interacting, protecting, supporting and raising our children.

Part of our healing as black men **must** be to re-institute fatherhood as a top priority for those of us who are fathers. Simply biologically producing a baby is not fatherhood. This is an act of nature. A brother could be the weakest lover in existence, incapable of the intimate sharing and pleasing of a woman, yet still produce life. In fact, rapists often impregnate their victims, so there should no longer be chest-beating or bragging about biologically co-creating a life with another. It *is* a miracle and a gift, but the work of being a father really goes into effect once the child is born.

We must also understand as fathers that our behavior is observed constantly by our children. In fact, they don't think about it, they simply *emulate, imitate, and duplicate* behavior. "Do as I say, not as I do" simply does not work. Our sons partially define manhood by our behavior, and our daughters often seek mates based on our behavior. If that behavior is merely a disappearing act, that model applies as well.

Black fatherhood: more challenging than it's ever been

Being a black father today is more difficult than it has ever been. Today, we are just coming to the realization of hundreds of years of trauma that we have passed on as "culture." At least our ancestors had a pretty clear understanding of their situation. We cannot insult their sacrifices by comparing them to what we deal with today; yet, things are more complicated now.

Some challenges:

- Due to our absence in the majority of black children's lives, black fathers are often viewed as unnecessary, the exception rather than the rule, an unwanted obstacle. In fact, since many black women have been raised without fathers, they have little understanding of the value of a *true* black father (this isn't to blame them, for they were forced to grow up with our abandonment).
- The whole labor force has changed. A semi-skilled black man can no longer support his family the way he could have 30 or more years ago.
- Drugs, including heroin, crack, fortified marijuana and malt liquor—by design or default—have been allowed to take root in our communities, resulting in the deterioration we currently see.
- The Black Church no longer is the hub of the black community, and has fallen out of touch with many of the core needs of our communities.
- The media has a stronger influence over our children (and us) than ever before in history, with negative consequences. Also, we perpetuate more of the negativity upon ourselves than ever before.
- There are more gangs, guns, violence, materialism, consumerism, drugs, corruption, disease, and other pitfalls than there have ever been.
- Our educational system—never designed with the best interests of black people—has become more inept and dysfunctional than ever.
- The number of incarcerated black men is higher than it has ever been, contributing greatly to the deterioration of black families and communities nationwide.
- Our self-concept as black people is more distorted and self-damaging than at anytime in our existence.

Today, it takes a strong desire, skill and great effort to be the type of father who can help our children through the many traps awaiting them. If we make conscious choices about our behavior with our children in mind, they can avoid these traps—even if we have been caught up in them in the past. Some of the things we should consider are:

> **If I'm currently involved in the criminal justice system, I've already increased the chances that my children will be.**
>
> **If I drink or use drugs, I have already increased the chances that my children will do so.**
>
> **If I am physically or verbally abusive towards women, my sons will likely be abusive, and my daughters will likely be in relationships where they'll be abused.**

My children may get their work ethic from me. If I am unable or unwilling to work, if I am regularly looking for a hustle, or if I'm "livin' up under some woman," my children will likely grow to have the same lack of a work ethic.

If I read, I am passing on this value to my children. If I don't, I am likewise passing that value on.

If I believe in education of self, my children will benefit from this, if not, they won't.

If I love, cherish and respect black women, my sons will do likewise and my daughters will settle for nothing less.

If I know who I am as a black man & father, my children will benefit. If I don't, it makes it more difficult for them to discover who they are and what they can be.

If I love, show affection, protect, mentor and teach my children, this will offset much of the damage that is done to them.

Especially for teen/young fathers:

If you are a young brother who has unexpectedly or intentionally become a father, there are some very important things you need to know:

- As you've heard before, aside from those men with a medical condition, any male can produce a baby with a woman. A real man provides physical, emotional and financial support for his child regardless of the status of his relationship with the child's mother.
- Infants and children are murdered, disabled and beaten every day. Often, the crime is committed by a young father, step-father or boyfriend who lacks the patience, self-control and maturity required to raise a child. If you <u>ever</u> feel like hitting or shaking an infant, remove yourself from the setting or seek help before you do some irreparable damage (physically or otherwise) to the child.
- Many teen fathers were without fathers—or any positive male figure—themselves. If you fall into this category, you had no role model to show you the love, patience and commitment required as a father. It will take some work to learn these traits.
- Enroll in a parenting class. There are some specifically for black men with children. Being a good father requires more skill, knowledge, patience, love and giving than anything else you'll do in your life
- Talk to a brother you know who *is* a truly responsible father, even one who's children are grown. They will have invaluable experience for you.
- Despite our collective failure as black men in this area, there is no greater sign of true manhood, courage or act of love than being a real father or father figure to our children.

Let our work begin—or continue—as the case may be.

MALE/FEMALE RELATIONSHIPS

The fact that the adult American Negro female emerges a formidable character is often met with amazement, distaste and even belligerence. It is seldom accepted as an inevitable outcome of the struggle won by survivors, and deserves respect if not enthusiastic acceptance.
--Maya Angelou

We don't love them hoes.
--Snoop Dogg

Brothers, we have to take a long, hard look within ourselves and examine our attitudes and treatment of black women. Abuse, exploitation and disrespect of ALL women are important issues we need to look at, but the dynamics between black men and women should take top priority.

Did you know?

- As a group, black women are at the bottom in terms of income in America, therefore they rank #1 for those living in poverty (in part, because of our lack of support, and contrary to those brothers who are always crying about "black women getting all the jobs").*

- While HIV is decreasing slightly among other segments of America's population, black women are the fastest growing group for HIV infection. The majority are infected through sexual intercourse with black men.**

- It is now estimated that nearly 70% of black children live in homes without fathers. In 70% of those cases, it is the mothers who are raising our children, with an increasing number of grandmothers and other extended family members.***

- If a black woman dies tonight through some type of homicide, there is an approximately 90% chance that it will be a black man who takes her life.

- Black women are the only group of people in America whose life expectancy actually decreases if they are married.****

- Sexual abuse and exploitation of black women and children is just as prevalent among black people as it is within America's general population.*****

There might be no way to measure these, but using your own personal knowledge or common sense, ask yourself: How many black women…

>…are addicted to crack, alcohol or some other substance that they used for the first time with a brother?

>…were sexually abused as a child by a black man - uncle, brother, step-brother, cousin or step-father?

>…have been cussed out, called names, ridiculed or disrespected by a brother?

>…have been hit by a black man?

>…contracted some STD (including HIV) from a brother?

>…have been cheated on by a brother to whom they had given their love?

What's your history?

Brothers, there is no shame in owning up to our faults; the shame comes when we are unwilling to look at the damage we have been subjected to and pass onto others. If you have gotten this far, you obviously have some belief that we have undergone trauma that needs to be brought to light, self-hatred we need to heal from and the resulting damage we pass onto others we need to reconcile.

When we don't feel like we're whole people, it is easier to take that humanity away from another person. In part to combat a low self-concept or self-esteem, we look for ways to get "one-up" on somebody else. With brothers, it leads to distrust and fights, but with sisters, more often we turn to control, abuse and sexual predation (trying to "hunt" for as many conquests as possible).

During the 1960s, people everywhere were challenging and rejecting traditional ideas about a variety of things such as race, gender and the roles they play in our lives. During that time, the idea of the "playboy" came into popularity. Being a man was linked to our sexual relationships. Just as women were rejecting the idea that they were only mothers and homemakers, men began to push away the idea that masculinity was measured in the way they protected and provided for their families. This was important for the masses because it allowed the definition of a "real man" to include those poor men who before couldn't measure up with their bank accounts.

Since black men—then just as now—represented higher levels of unemployment and often worked in jobs that paid less, many jumped at this opportunity to prove their worth, and jumped into this sexual arena in attempts to manufacture self-esteem. To this day, we continue to embrace the idea of being a pimp or a player as positive attributes, using them in greetings and compliments ("What's up, playa?" "He's a pimp for that."). We accept them and ignore the way those values break down our integrity and further erode our self-esteem. Despite what we say and do, many of us really would like to be faithful and committed, but instead pretend those values don't matter to us. Since we can't hide from our true feelings for long, the actual result is a lowered self-image and further blows to our already eroding self-esteem.

Ask Yourself:

Have I ever cheated on a woman I truly cared for?

If so, what thoughts did I have about myself or the situation during that time?

If it was in the past, have my thoughts changed since then?

Because of our distorted sense of manhood, we often look at sensitive brothers as weak or inferior. But true strength lies in being able to be in touch with our whole selves—emotionally, physically, and spiritually. When we can see our entire self, we are more likely to be able to see others as whole too, and as a result, be less likely to try to hustle or victimize them. To do so requires some work on building up our self-concept.

In the movie *The Color Purple*, based on the book by Alice Walker, we follow the character Celie, who undergoes a lifetime of abuse from the men in her life—father and husband alike. At one point, when she decides she's taken enough, she tells her husband, "Everything you do to me, already been done to you." This statement holds true in real life. Often we cheat on our partners because we feel we've been cheated. We disrespect them because we feel disrespected. We abuse them because we feel beat down. When we do our own work to heal and grow, we will be in good position to reverse some of the damage we have caused—to make amends, and work on building stronger families again.

What is your current relationship status (married, single, divorced, monogamous relationship, dating multiple women)?

_____

If you are currently in a relationship, how would you describe it?

_____

_____

If you are not in a relationship currently, but would like to be, describe the type of relationship you would like to have.

_____

_____

What are the 10 qualities you feel are most important in a relationship?

_____   _____

_____   _____

_____   _____

_____   _____

_____   _____

Describe how you feel about black women.

_____

_____

_____

Have you ever grabbed, pushed, threatened or hit a black woman?
Why?

_____

_____

_____

Under what circumstances would you do so now?

_____

_____

_____

Do you feel there is any reason that justifies hitting a black woman or using any type of physical force?

_____

_____

_____

Have you ever cussed a black woman out or called her out of her name?

_____

Put an 'X' next to the character traits you feel generally apply to black women:

___Beautiful	___Loving	___Demanding	___Angry	___Sexy
___Intelligent	___Strong	___Promiscuous	___Fun	___Hard
___Materialistic	___Depressed	___Sensitive	___Caring	___Smart
___Responsible	___Loose	___Frigid	___Funny	___Ugly
___Perceptive	___Violent	___Cold	___Sweet	___Shy

This was kind of a trick question, brothers. Any of these traits could be attributed to individual women of all races. It should be impossible to assign characteristics like these to entire groups. If you marked the standard negative stereotyped traits often used against black women like Materialistic, Hard, Loose or Angry, it actually says more about *us* and our perception of black women than it does the sisters themselves. It also speaks to the way black women are portrayed in our society, and the way we buy into those portrayals.

Sometimes as black men we get so consumed by our own experiences, we fail to look at the reality of sisters. For example:

- They are the primary parent for the majority of our children, often raising them without our support.
- Black women were systemically raped by white men for hundreds of years long before it was recognized as rape.
- Routinely raised white children as well as their own children.
- Have been undyingly loyal to black men, while we have not been so with them.
- Gave birth to us, taught us, loved us and raised us, often without the support of our fathers.
- In a society designed primarily to favor white males, they are at the bottom facing racism AND sexism.
- Have become the backbone of what is left of black communities, being the sole providers for too many of our children.
- They are the mothers of civilization, dating back to the early humans in East Africa.
- Have routinely been the conscious of America, from Harriet Tubman to Rosa Parks and millions of others.
- They are the epitome of beauty, even though America has programmed us to think the opposite.
- Despite countless violations at the hands of America and US, continue to love, be vulnerable with, fight for and with, and share their souls with us.

- Despite being our primary victims in HIV/AIDS/STD transmission, homicide, domestic violence, infidelity, abandonment, sexual abuse & assault, they have NEVER given up on us.
- Love us, fight for justice, defend what is right, and protect our people like no one else can
- As mothers, girlfriends, and wives, they routinely stay committed to us even when we are incarcerated (Ironically, at a women's prison, you also see many black women visitors, but few brothers).
- Despite a history of often being brutalized sexually, physically, economically, psychologically, emotionally by white AND black men, they have continually represented the essence of beauty, love, strength, creativity and perseverance.

We have to admit brothers. Black women are remarkable. Nothing against women of other races, for if we are in a partnership with any woman, we are called to give all of the love, commitment and respect they deserve.

A great deal of work to do...TOGETHER

As you know, this book is about healing, redefining and reclaiming black manhood. However, we can not do so in a vacuum. While we can spend days extolling the qualities of black women, it would be foolish not to realize that our sisters have also been traumatized and damaged by our history in America. Having never spent a day as a woman, we, the authors of this publication, in the theme of self-responsibility decided we could only focus on ourselves as black men. It is up to the sisters to decide if and how they choose to redefine black womanhood.

Because of our unique history, the absence of many brothers in our communities and children's lives, we can not heal our relationship with black women according to our own perceptions. This must be done WITH the sisters. Some things have changed in the majority of black families while many of us have been gone. As you can imagine, it would be insulting in our quest to reestablish our presence among our people, to fail to recognize that in our absence, the sisters have been handling their business along with ours.

This isn't to say that scandalous behavior does not exist with sisters. To be sure, black women are in just as much need for healing. However, we as black men must come correct before we call on others to do so.

DOMESTIC VIOLENCE
Including Sexual Assault & Child Abuse

For those of us who hit, slap, grab, push, threaten or intimidate women, 1 of 3 things is probably going on with us:

1. I am extremely insecure, afraid and underdeveloped emotionally.
2. I have a very serious anger problem and easily lose control (reptilian brain).
3. I came from a family where physical abuse was practiced.

Men who abuse women do so for control. We like to control, humiliate, dominate and objectify women because it makes us feel less insecure about ourselves. To treat women in such a way is similar to how our ancestors were treated as slaves. In fact, men who abuse women have more in common with the slave masters who "owned" our ancestors than we would like to admit:

- Objectify and dehumanize another to justify ones inhumane treatment of them (through labels, name-calling, stereotypes and generalizations)
- Fear of blacks was required to own slaves, fear of powerlessness and control is required to abuse women
- Seriously damaged self-esteem is needed to dehumanize another human being
- One has to be out of touch with, or lacking in humanity to enslave another or abuse a woman
- Insecurity. A truly secure person would not want to "own" another person, or "control" their spouse/partner

As black men we have been objectified and dehumanized historically. We have also been marginalized and struggle with self-esteem issues. We also often present an excess of bravado that really hides deep-seated insecurities.

We aren't saying that these facts make us more prone to abuse women, but it can. While other cultures are male-dominated, some of us have taken the practice of abusing and exploiting women to new highs – or rather, lows. The "pimp" mentality is one example of this as well as the "playa" that is looked at as the ultimate man for his ability to exploit and manipulate women sexually and financially.

Remember the old story about the poor working stiff who is regularly ridiculed by his boss, then comes home and beats his wife and kids, and kicks his dog? Many humans are guilty of similar behavior. When we feel powerless, we subconsciously take out our frustrations or exercise power over those who are safest to do so with, or those who can't fight back.

Have you ever taken out your anger on someone who didn't have anything to do with why you were angry?

131

When engaged in a heated argument, did the other person's fear of you increase your anger and cause you to be even more intimidating?

Have you ever said to yourself "She deserved to get hit," "she brought it on herself," or some such statement?

Truth is, she **never** deserves to be hit. Those of us who think so have some serious issues within ourselves. Those of us who know it's wrong to hit women, but lose control and do so have serious issues with anger and rage we need to come to terms with. Everyday, 3 women in the United States are murdered at the hands of their spouses. Some of those were intentional, but some were caused by the same temporary loss of control some of us experience.

Domestic violence is the second leading cause for incarceration of black men besides drug offenses. Brothers, we got problems.

What can I do?

- Do a self-analysis. Do you have a habit of hitting, pushing, threatening, or putting your hands on women? If so, get some help. You can do so now of your own accord or wait until the courts require you to do so.
- Examine your own family history. Was domestic violence present in your family? Were you beaten as a child? How did the men in your family relate to women?
- Conduct an emotional self-check. Men are socialized (programmed) to avoid expressing any emotions except anger. Are you able to identify when you are afraid, vulnerable, insecure, sad, angry or hurt? Many of us can't get ourselves to say such a thing out loud. Is it any wonder we are unable to identify or express any emotion other than anger?
- Go to a support group. There are Men's Groups specifically designed to deal with abusive behavior. Again, you can look into the problem on your own, or let the problem grow until you are court-ordered to do so.
- Examine your attitudes toward women. When you interact with women is sex on your mind? Are you able to view women as people? Do you have female friends?
- Visit a setting where you can communicate with women who have been victims of domestic violence. Such places are often kept secret because we as men stalk and kill so many of the women we say we love. But there are public forums available where the victims tell their stories.
- Examine the attitudes of your peers regarding women. If one of your partners calls a woman a bitch or brags about "gettin paid" by women, do you challenge their views of women or go along to be accepted?

Somewhere along the line, many of us as black men have begun to view it as a sign of manhood to treat women the same way or worse than the slave masters did. Abuse of any kind against women isn't about them, it's about us. And it shows itself in many ways:

Jealousy. Being insecure about her interactions with other men. We won't see it as insecurity, we'll probably call it "being disrespected". But its always about how we view ourselves.

Financial control. Keep her without money. For many of us this comes out when we refuse to pay child support for our kids. We often accuse her of spending the money wrong, partying with it, or "spending it on another nigga" but it comes down to us trying to exercise financial control, and using our children as ransom.

Isolation. We may not like this friend of hers, or don't want her going out with that friend. In reality, we are insecure, and are afraid she'll see how little we think of ourselves and find someone better. Again, this isn't about her, it's about us.

Threats. Brothers, what pleasure can one really get by threatening someone we outweigh by 100 lbs. and tower over? Do we really want a woman to be with us because she is afraid of us?

Guilt. We threaten suicide. We tell her she's dogging our kids and our family. We tell her we are nothing without her, and don't see the point of going on. This is dangerous. These individuals are the ones who can murder their own children to hurt her, or take the "if I can't have you, no one will" approach. It happens, every day.

No offense, but for those of you who think it's alright to force sex on a woman because, "even though she said no, I could tell she really wanted it", this book can't help you. What you are doing isn't about black manhood, or even a distorted self-concept of black manhood. You are a rapist. Get help as soon as possible. If you don't, you need to be locked up so you can't hurt anyone else.

For those who sexually abuse children, or even some of you older brothers who lustfully look at young women or girls, we are telling you man-to-man, it ain't normal and something is wrong with you. You need more help than this book even comes close to providing. The rest of us need to stand up, speak out against physical abuse, sexual assault and child molestation. Truth be told, we need to protect the community from you.

ACTION STEPS:

Review history. Think about all those traumas that have taken place during our history - rape, physical, verbal & emotional abuse, the inability of black men to protect black women and children and <u>all</u> of the feelings that created, and how black women were viewed. Read historical books written by black women to gain insight on their perspective. Imagine what it would have been like for black women as wives, mothers, sisters and daughters. Then, through videos and sitcoms, examine how black women are portrayed today.

Talk to black women. Whether it be your wife, girlfriend, mother, grandmother, sister, daughter or co-worker, ask for their perspective on black male/female relationships. Ask them what are the most difficult parts of being a black woman. What do they value in a relationship? What are their values, goals, priorities and dreams? What do they think of black men? Ask about their hurts, pain and betrayals.

Analyze media portrayals of women. Next time you are watching television, study how women – especially black women – are portrayed. Count the number of times there is some level of sexual suggestiveness. Just because the women play the rolls, don't be fooled. The media is controlled by men, and like us as black people, they portray women the way they want to view them.

Anger management. If you have a problem with anger, go check out a group or even by a book about it. As men, we are trained to be aggressive. Some of us take it to the extreme. Exploring the source of our anger problem will reduce our stress, lengthen our lives, help our children learn what healthy relationships are, and heal our wounds. What are the emotions behind the anger? Can I identify them? Am I able to talk to any of my friends about them? If you can't be the real you with your friends, maybe it is time to find new friends.

Speak out against abuse. As black people, we often expect whites to do the right thing. As men we need to do the same. There is nothing manly about abusing or exploiting women. It is actually pretty cowardly when you think about it. The media and videos feed us a constant diet of women being objectified, sexualized and exploited. It will take great effort on our part to put forth a message that pimping, slapping women and taking advantage of them financially is not something that black men do – at least not real men.

Surround yourself with like-minded brothers. Truth is, you surround yourself with those who share the same values as you do. If you can't respect women in the presence of your peer group, it's probably not their fault, it's on you. When you examine your own attitudes about women and correct them, those cats may cut you loose.

Recognize sexual addiction. As we've said before, historically many of us as black men did not have equal access to traditional forms of feeling good about ourselves, so we developed alternatives. "I may not have a job, but the ladies love my black ass." is basically what it amounts to. Many of us use conquest of women to feel better about ourselves. Some of us use sex like a drug. We try to get lost in the pleasure and excited by the game of pursuit. Others among us have taken it to an even deeper level with pornography, prostitutes and strip clubs. There is such a thing as sexual addiction, and there are 12 Step programs throughout the country to help deal with it. Besides, unprotected sex and the subsequent spreading of HIV is one of the ways we as black men place a death sentence on black women.

Black male/female support & healing group. Be a part of a Black Male/Female Healing & Support Group. If there isn't one where you are, get together with some people and start one. With all the hurt, trauma, anger, resentment, tension and pain that exist between black men and women, there is no reason for us not to talk to each other.

De-program ourselves. As men, we have all been socialized to varying degrees to objectify women, which makes abuse more acceptable. Recovery from this programming won't take place over night, it is a life-long process. But we can begin now.

Help our children. Many of our children practice the act of abuse early in their lives based on our examples and the constant images they see through the media. We need to begin having serious discussions with our children about where this behavior comes from. Fred Sanford and his sister-in-law, Aunt Ester, JJ and his sister Thelma and George Jefferson and his housekeeper and neighbor are but a few examples of verbal abuse and physical threats many of us grew up to and laughed at. No men threaten to physically beat women to laughs the way we do. The abusive verbal exchanges between black men and women have become legendary. Like "soul food", this is an element of our so-called culture based on self-hatred and we need to reject it.

Sexual slavery. Women and children around the world are being sold into slavery. And yes, it happens here in the United States. As black men we need to put our own houses in order, but we also need to become active in this horrific practice. As black men we often don't have a voice. Here is an opportunity to undertake our own healing and lead men in combating one of the most exploitive, sick and dehumanizing practices in existence.

Part 7
THE CRIMINAL JUSTICE SYSTEM

"More than any other single public policy, America's crime control industry magnifies and exacerbates racial inequality, deepens black poverty, and wreaks widespread destabilization on black families, and communities."

--Bruce Dixon, *The Black Commentator*

INCARCERATION
America's Rite of Passage for Black Males

You could abort every black baby in this country and the crime rate would go down.
> --Former Education Secretary William Bennett during his nationally-syndicated radio show.

Simply put, white cops are afraid of black men. We don't talk about it, we pretend it doesn't exist, we claim "color blindness," we say white officers treat black men the same way they treat white men. But that's a lie. In fact, the bigger, the darker the black man the greater the fear. The African American community knows this. Hell, most whites know it.
> --Former Seattle Police Department Chief Norm Stamper, *Breaking Rank*

Most of us are aware of the realities of America's criminal justice system, but as a reminder:

We know law enforcement agencies focus a disproportionate amount of their resources in communities of color. Crimes that blacks may engage in (street drug sales, crack cocaine) receive more aggressive enforcement than those crimes generally committed by whites (identity theft, prescription drug markets, powder cocaine, larger drug trade, corporate crimes). These crimes also receive stiffer penalties upon conviction.

Most law enforcement officers are inadequately selected and trained to maintain positive relationships with black communities. Most police departments feign attempts at bridging these gaps by hiring more black officers. Since black officers are selected and trained using the same criteria as white officers, they don't necessarily bring improved relationships with black people. Their job depends on them upholding the values of the system in which they work. As a result, they can make the situation worse.

In poor communities and communities of color, the over-emphasized police presence combined with the negative interpersonal interactions causes an adversarial relationship between the police and the community. This is even highlighted among those law-abiding residents of those neighborhoods, as underscored nationally with high-profile cases like Rodney King, Amadou Diallo, Patrick Dorismond, Abner Louima and Robert Lee Thomas Sr., where black men who have been shot, tortured or beaten by white officers with no consequence in most of the cases.

Studies have long-shown that a white man and black man with identical criminal histories and charged with the same crime will receive consistently different sentences, with the black man usually receiving the harsher penalty, from low-level drug possession charges all the way up to capital crimes and death row sentencing.

Some sobering statistics:

- As of December 31, 2004, there were 2,135,901 people in the United States in prisons or jails. *
- For males only, blacks are incarcerated at a rate of 4,919 per 100,000 compared to 717 per 100,000 for whites. *
- For black males ages of 25 - 29, the incarceration rate is 12,603 per 100,000 compared to 1,666 per 100,000 for white males 25 – 29. Consequently, 12.6% of black men in their late 20s are currently incarcerated. *
- Widely recognized as one of the most racist nations in recent history, South Africa during apartheid (1993) South Africa incarcerated 851 black males per 100,000 compared to the 4,919 per 100,000 incarceration rate of black males in the U.S. as of 12/31/2004.* This is almost 6x less than in our supposedly free nation.
- Nearly 5% of all black men, compared to 0.6% of white men, are incarcerated. ****

Locally:

- Black people account for 8.4% of Seattle's population, and 5.4% of King County's population (Ironically, King County is officially named Martin Luther King County). **
- Blacks make up 39.8% of all incarcerated people in Martin Luther King County. ***
- Blacks represent 3.2% of the general population of Washington state, yet 18.1% of all those incarcerated in Washington state. ****

Taking responsibility

You don't need us to tell you that the criminal justice system is biased in America. It always has been and will likely continue to be so. It doesn't mean we give up on the battle to change these systems, but we will be in a better position to combat the inequities while we are free of warrants, indictments and incarceration. As the above stats show, there are some awful truths about how legislation is passed, selective enforcement of certain laws and the racist nature of the system. But we are interested in first addressing the actions we take that make us prey for such an imbalanced institution. Therefore, as a first step, we should first look at what we've done to put ourselves in situations where we are charged and incarcerated?

*Sources: Washington DC: Human Rights Watch, June 2000 **U.S. Census /Bureau 2000 *** King County Department of Adult & Juvenile Detention, 2005 **** US Bureau of Justice Statistics 2004

Have you ever…

Been charged with a crime?

_____

_____

Did you do any time as a result?

_____

_____

Have you ever been on probation or parole?

_____

_____

What were the crimes you were placed on probation or parole for?

_____

_____

Have you ever been charged with violating your probation or parole?

_____

_____

What were the consequences of the violation(s)?

_____

_____

Have you ever had warrants issued against you for unpaid parking/traffic tickets?

_____

_____

What specifically were the tickets for?

How did you resolve these tickets? Did you do time or pay money? If so, how much time and/or money?

Have you ever, or do you currently have a suspended license?

Have you ever been charged with domestic violence? If so, who were you accused of assaulting, and what were the consequences?

What were the results/consequences of these charges? Did you do time? Ordered to go to Anger Management? How much did it cost you financially? Were you under court supervision for any period of time as a result?

Have you ever been charged with possession of drugs?

What about possession with intent to deliver?

_____

_____

What were the consequences?

_____

_____

Depending on your answers, you can see we often put ourselves in the hands of the judicial system by our own deeds. Is America's judicial system biased? Of course it is. In fact, we should stop debating that fact with those who fail—or refuse—to see it. Instead, we need to understand how the system is biased, then spend our energies assuring that our own behavior doesn't place us in the grips of such a system.

For example, if we believe we may become the victim of racial profiling in traffic stops, then why would we roll in an uninsured car full of weed smoke? Regardless of the reason the officer pulled us over, the end result justifies his bias in the eyes of the system. In this case, the result is multiple citations for possession of a controlled substance and driving without insurance, as well as a license to search the vehicle. In his song "99 Problems," Jay-Z says, "I ain't passed the bar but I know a little bit." We should heed his advice: understand your rights _and_ responsibilities—taking care that we don't put ourselves in a position to be detained, arrested and run through the criminal justice system.

We can and should continue to fight for REAL justice in our criminal justice system, but that fight should not include overlooking, excusing or denying our own behaviors and values as black men.

Re-read the core elements of black manhood list at the end of this book. What do these words mean to you?

_____

_____

Are they important characteristics you feel should be at the core of every man's self-concept?

_____

_____

If so, provide some specific examples of how you have chosen to integrate these characteristics into your self-concept.

_____

_____

_____

_____

Sociological theory suggests that when a person or groups of people are denied access to something they need or value, they will develop alternate ways of reaching that goal. Throughout our history, we often were denied the ability to exhibit our manhood and gain respect in traditional ways (working, education, protecting our families & communities, business ownership…), so we have developed alternative ways of defining ourselves as men. As Dr. Joy DeGruy-Leary points out in her book, *Post Traumatic Slave Syndrome*, we as black men go to great extremes trying to capture the respect America has consistently denied us. The problem is, these extremes have resulted in us compromising elements of decency and humanity. Many of them also cause us to run afoul of the law. Some examples:

- Pimping
- Selling drugs
- Domestic violence
- Exercising control over women as if they are property
- Neglecting & abandoning our children
- Extreme materialism
- Rejecting social norms in favor of *alternative* or *street* rules (often no rules at all, or survival of the fittest)
- A "gangsta" mentality and lifestyle
- Extreme violence and gun play as options to resolve conflict

Once again, this isn't to say that these behaviors are exclusive to black men. It also is not to say that America's justice system is not racist at its core. Prison reform is necessary, but we have to do something to dramatically decrease the number of black lives entering the system. This is not to say that it's our entire fault, but that we can take responsibility for the part that is ours. In the minds of many of us, though, America's inhumanity towards us historically is beyond measure, therefore, we often excuse ourselves, and choose to focus on the behavior of those who have oppressed us. If we instead work on the issues that are ours at the core, we will have more warriors to fight those important battles that need fighting.

144

THE CRACK EPIDEMIC

The streets is a short stop. Either you slingin' crack rock, or you got a wicked jump shot.
>--Notorious B.I.G.

In his song, "Things Done Changed," Biggie reiterated a philosophy held by so many young black men who grow up in poverty. The drug game, sports, and rap music have become viewed as the only ways to get out of the ghetto. Since there are only about 400 men in the NBA at any given moment, and major record label contracts are almost as elusive, the crack game often seems like the best road to riches. The problem is, as noted above, the prisons are filling up with men who have been duped into believing that same lie.

Many have argued that the crack industry itself was invented in a conspiracy to make a few people rich and to further cripple poor black communities. Others have said it pointed to it as a means to fill the growing prison industry. With so many of our families being destroyed by a single product (by loss of family member due to its use or by incarceration due to its sale), it is probably prudent to at least have some basic understanding of its history and context.

How did we get here?

In the mid 1980s, several forces converged at the same time to result in the current state of incarceration in many communities.   One of the biggest factors was the economic policy of then-president Ronald Reagan. Reganomics, as it became known, was an adaptation of supply-side economics, which followed a theory that by cutting taxes for big business and deregulating domestic trade markets, corporations would lower prices and create jobs for the working class, thus making the economy stronger. In actuality, we found that most of those corporations just took the profits and ran, and the wealth that was supposed to "trickle down" never made it to the lower segments of society.

In order to pay for the tax cuts to business, Reganomics had to make cuts to social spending—schools, welfare, unemployment, etc. As a result, as the economy stagnated, some factories were closed to increase profits, worker retraining programs were limited and drug use grew, there were no programs to aid those most affected. Ask those old enough to remember how many homeless people they saw before the Reagan era. Likely, not many.

With 12 years of Reaganomics (2 terms by Reagan, 1 by his vice-president George Bush senior) from 1980-1992, most of us reading this book are products of that economic system. It was the era that saw the motto "Greed is Good" form the ethics of Wall Street, and that greed carried over into even the poorest neighborhoods. But that greed needed a different product to fuel the market. That product came to be crack cocaine.

According to *Encyclopedia of Drugs: Cocaine, A New Epidemic*, by Chris-Ellyn Johanson, the price of 1 kilogram of cocaine in 1981 was $55,000. Three years later, 1984, that price was down to $25,000.

If you follow the laws of supply and demand, such a dramatic drop in wholesale pricing must be the result of higher quantities of cocaine being available on the streets.

Where did such quantities come from, and where were they going?

It is probably no accident that cocaine began to proliferate in the United States during the 1980s. During that time, wars in Nicaragua and El Salvador were largely about control of Central America, the strategic halfway point for air travel between Colombia and the United States. At one point, the US supported the Contra War in Nicaragua, but when that aid was cut, covert operations led by Oliver North and his cohorts found other ways to supply the Contras—in part from drug dealing. Planes left the US with guns, left the guns in Central America, and returned to the US with cocaine. The Contra War against Sandinista Nicaragua, as well as the war against the national liberation forces in El Salvador, was largely about control of this critical area. When Congress cut off support for the Contras, Oliver North and friends found other ways to fund the Contra re-supply operations, in part through drug dealing.

According to a 1996 report, "The Dark Alliance," in the *San Jose Mercury News,* former Nicaraguan drug lord and current DEA informant, Danilo Blandon swore under oath that the drugs for weapons deal dumped thousands of kilos of cocaine into Los Angeles' African-American neighborhoods in the 1980s. The plan, hatched by the CIA, was largely to blame for the crack epidemic and the rise of the Crips and Bloods. According to Blandon, cut-rate cocaine was delivered to L.A.-area street gangs through a young, South-Central brother by the name of Ricky "Freeway Rick" Donnell Ross. Unaware of the military and political connections to his supply, Freeway Rick turned the powder cocaine into crack and wholesaled it to gangs across the country.

(You can read the full story at http://weekendinterviewshow.com/Darkalliance.html)

Neighborhoods in LA and elsewhere were not ready to deal with such an aggressively addictive drug and such an aggressive marketing plan. Almost overnight, crack was everywhere as street-level dealers were ready to follow Wall Street's promise of riches.

Chemical/Biological warfare: An American Tradition

Think the government would never result to such tactics? Think about the following incidents.

- Early European settlers intentionally infected blankets with yellow fever and small pox and gave the blankets to Native American tribes. Since the indigenous people (original inhabitants) hadn't been previously exposed to these diseases, and had no immunities to them. This was an intentional element of genocide against Native Americans. Native Americans had no tolerance to alcohol because of a lack of previous exposure. It wasn't long before the early European settlers discovered this and used it to their advantage in the genocide of Native people. The lasting effects of this chemical warfare are still apparent today among the Native people.

- During a forty year period—from 1932 to 1972—the US Department of Public Health studied 399 black men with syphilis. These men were never told that they had syphilis and were "studied" until their death. This was known as the Tuskegee Experiment.

- COINTELPRO (Counter Intelligence Program) was a covert strategy by the FBI and US government designed to prevent the unification of "radical" black individuals and organizations (Dr. King, Malcolm X, NAACP, SNCC - Student Non-Violence Coordinating Committee, Black Panther Party & others). We now know that one of their strategies was to flood black communities with heroin.

Hustlin' or being hustled?

Another diabolical facet of this history is that while the drug was taking root in our communities, legislation was simultaneously being drafted to feed the prison industry with those who were using and selling it. Reagan rode his War on Drugs to become one of the most popular presidents in American History. Part of that war on drugs was the 1986 Anti Drug Abuse Act, which made even relatively lower-level drug sales federal offenses, and offered up newly crafted mandatory minimum sentences. The result 20 years later is shown in jails and prisons bulging with young men and women serving time for relatively "minor" drug offenses.

We won't tell you to buy into every conspiracy theory that hits the streets, only to use the information available to you to decide for yourself. Some questions to consider:

- Has the United States been involved in covert operations to manipulate leadership of other governments?
- During the Iran-Contra affair, were weapons provided to the Contras of Nicaragua? What did they have to exchange for the weapons?
- Did this all take place around the same time that the crack cocaine epidemic hit black communities across America?
- How has the crack epidemic contributed to the rise in jail and prison populations?
- Over the last 20+ years, what has the crack cocaine epidemic done to black people? Black families and communities?
- What has been the impact on the growth of the Crips and Bloods?
- How has crack affected the level of violence in black communities?
- What affect has crack had on the number of black men imprisoned?

Whether or not your feel the conspiracy holds true, merely thinking through the origins and the effects of such crack in our communities has to cause a thinking person to pause. If you are now, or ever have been involved in this type of "hustle," does any of the information above change your thoughts about it? In fact, who exactly is doing the hustling?

PRISON INDUSTRIAL COMPLEX

California's Prison Industry Authority is like the goose that laid the golden egg. As long as no one kills the goose, PIA employees, and the myriad vendors who make a living supplying the prison industry continue getting the gold. The trouble is, though, the goose is crapping all over everyone else.
--Willie Wisely, California State Prisoner, writing in *The Bottom Line*

Without debate, the prison population is growing at incredible rates. In fact, data shows that the population in county, state and federal prisons and jails grows by over 54,000 each year, to a current total of 2 million people imprisoned in this country. The question is, are these criminals fueling the need to build more jails and prisons, or are we locking people up in order to fuel the growing prison industry?

The Big Business of Prisons

Prison pay phones can generate as much as $15,000 per year (about 5 times the typical revenue of a pay phone on the street. The big phone companies all have their own prison phone service, which they market heavily to prison officials and institution management. AT&T's service—called The Authority, Bell South's MAX and MCI's Maximum Security all target the perfect phone service customer: the phone is their most important link to the rest of the world, most of their communication is made by collect calls, and they can't shop for the carrier with the lowest rates.

The prison phone service is such a moneymaker for these companies that MCI installed its service in California jails and prisons at no charge to the state. They knew they could recoup their money from the inmates' calls. These phone companies have routinely been caught overcharging for calls, attaching high "service charges" not made to customers outside jails and prisons (as high as $3 per call some places), and even adding minutes to calls made by inmates.

Phone calls aren't the only business thriving at the expense of prisoners. If you're in an institution now, look around. You see uniforms, beds, security and surveillance equipment, food service, guards and corrections officers. The companies that make or provide those services don't do so for free. They are making high profits based on the need to lock you up.

Private prisons are thriving. Big companies like Allstate, American Express, Merrill Lynch and Shearson Lehman all have invested in companies that build prisons. Companies like Wackenhut and Corrections Corporation of America are thriving, thanks to mandatory minimum sentences and our willingness to live life on a hustle. If we compare the income of these prison executives with the average brother on the street, though, it's clear who is getting played.

These companies stay full thanks to another growing industry—that of the "Bed Broker." Like a national hotel reservation system, bed brokers shop the space available in these private prisons and market them to the overcrowded state systems around the country. The private institution then rent space to prisoners from around the country. In exchanges like this, the prison charges the state institution to lock up its prisoners, and the bed broker receives about 10% of that fee. In 1996, the Newton County Correctional Center in Texas, operated by a private company, became the State of Hawaii's third largest prison.

How many people do you know that have been imprisoned out of state for a crime committed locally? Chances are, they were filling a spot "reserved" by a bed broker.

The New Slavery

In order to compete with cheap third-world labor costs, many corporations have learned that prison labor power can help maximize their profit margin. IBM, Chevron, Motorola and Victoria's Secret are among the corporate giants that use prison labor for data entry, production and customer call-centers. Nordstrom department stores sell "Prison Blues" jeans made by inmates in Oregon State institutions. Graduation caps and gowns are made by prisoners in South Carolina. The prison labor is seen as a windfall by corporations. The workers can't unionize or strike. Health benefits and unemployment insurance costs are gone. These corporations are able to decrease costs and increase production, making the bottom line dollar figure much more attractive to shareholders.

While private prisons are the most foul in regards to prisoners pay, even state and federal prisons pay laborers far less than minimum wage. While a worker in federal prison might earn as much as $1.25 per hour, at the highest paying private prison, CCA in Tennessee, pay tops out at 50 cents per hour—and that only for "highly skilled positions."

Much the same way America grew from a British colony to the richest country in the world by using free (slave) labor to grow its economy, American companies are driving their competitors out of business by using prison labor. Prisoners work for pennies because they have no rights. Even the 14th Amendment which abolished slavery excludes prisoners from its protections. As a result, wages of 20 cents per hour are not uncommon.

> **In your lifetime, have you refused to apply for a job that you thought was degrading or paid too little? If so, what kind of job was it?**

_____

_____

_____

> **Did you think about or resort to illegal means to generate income instead? What kind of hustle was it?**

_____

_____

_____

How many dollars would you need to make hustling to be worth 5 years of your life building furniture for 23 cents per hour *(5 years is the mandatory minimum sentence in federal court for 5 grams of crack cocaine)***?**

_____

_____

_____

As you can see, there are so many incentives for government and business to conspire to fill our prisons. Think about how many police man-hours go into a simple buy-bust, or how many people you know that have been locked up for possessing a minimal amount of weed or crack. Brothers, your freedom is much more important than a few dollars—especially dollars that we tend to spend as soon as we get them. We need to value our lives more, realize that traps exist for us in the world, and then do whatever is in our power to avoid those traps. Getting caught up in a short-sighted hustle at the expense of our future is one trap we need to learn to avoid.

INCORPORATING OUR TRAUMA
Other Institutions Profiting from Our Ills

Little attention is paid to the plight of black men and the criminal justice system. While we wait for America to realize the un-justness of its justice system, our people continue to be warehoused. America has yet to officially acknowledge and apologize for slavery, so history shows us that waiting for America to resolve that which it created is likely a fruitless labor. To continue to do so is a form of psychological slavery to say the least.

At one time, the black community was much more effective and dealing with our own issues. During those times, we developed and supported our own businesses. We addressed the needs of financially, spiritually and emotionally needy through churches, neighbors and extended families. And we policed our own behaviors through the village concept—adults would call us on our inappropriate behavior.

Not only have our communities fragmented, the power of addressing our problems has been taken out of the community and privatized. Agencies nationwide are profiting on our poverty and marginalization. Some of the industries are those that allege to address:

- Mental health treatment
- Chemical dependency treatment
- Mental health counseling
- Anger management
- Gang intervention
- Mentorship programs
- Family counseling
- Adolescent counseling
- Recreation
- Homelessness

- Mental illness
- Special education
- Boot camps
- Detention
- Diversion
- Probation/parole officers
- Tutoring
- Job readiness
- Criminal justice system

There is nothing wrong with these services in and of themselves, but there is something wrong when we as black people have allowed ourselves to be marginalized from working on our own behalf. Some examples:

> At one time not too long ago, black men who were in recovery from drug and/or alcohol addiction discovered something. They found that not only could they continue to work on their own recovery, but also they had a gift and passion to help others to achieve recovery. It required taking certified courses on pharmacology, counseling, family systems, case management, and a few others. These days that work is no longer in the hands of those men and women. The State requires advanced degrees and different certification requirements. Those with often minor criminal offenses (which includes most former drug abusers) are also now prohibited from working in the field. As a result, fewer black men are allowed to work in the profession that helped get them clean and sober, passing that gift onto others.

151

Similar to the chemical dependency field, the mental health field has undergone some changes in recent years. Many counseling and case management positions have been replaced by positions requiring a Masters degree. And even as fewer blacks are able to work in the field, they now often need a white supervisor to sign off on their work with black children, families, or groups. This "expert" qualification in African American culture is based on a training program, not demonstrated competency or life experience. In theory, a black counselor as skilled as Asa Hilliard or bell hooks would have to get a so-called expert like Dr. Phil to sign off on their work with black families.

Mental health agencies often now rank their clients based on a difficulty scale to obtain Medicare/Medicaid matching funds. For example, someone rated as a 1-A regarding their mental diagnosis, may generate $50.00 per hour to work with. A 3-B diagnosis is said to be more severe, therefore generating reimbursement at the rate of $62.00 (*dollar amounts are not actual, but used for comparison purposes*). Since mental health professionals have no diagnostic tools specifically to measure the marginalization, alienation and distorted self-concept one might have based on being black in America, it is a certainty that many of our people—kids and adults alike—are being misdiagnosed. I'm sure there are instances (conscious or subconscious) where a diagnosis is more severe than it needs to be in order to generate a larger reimbursement.

The DSM IV (Diagnostic Statistical Manual) is basically the Bible that mental health professionals are required to use before a mental, behavioral or personality diagnosis can be made. There is *nothing* in the DSM IV that speaks to the black experience in America, even though blacks are disproportionately diagnosed through schools, mental health facilities and the criminal justice system.

One area where you may never find a shortage of blacks, especially black men, are in the roles of police officers, correction officers for youth and adults and from the local jail to the federal prison and various forms of security guards. This presents the perception that the criminal justice system is unbiased: while they may lock up a disproportionate number of blacks, they also hire a great number of us. Problem is, due to the culture of law enforcement along with the selection process, blacks in the profession may be as unenlightened as their white peers in the racial dynamics of our justice system. Very few of them are in any position to change the culture, and as a result, the system is perpetuated.

Clearly, the problems we face provide a comfortable income for many people. Rather than waiting for these outside institutions to cure us, it is imperative that we take that job on ourselves. If we don't man-up now, it's possible that we never will.

ACTION STEPS

Principles. Each one of us needs to adopt a clear set of principles. The "getting paid by any means necessary" and "get rich or die trying" mentalities are killing us and deteriorating our spirit. We understand that there are many external forces that impact our lives, but that is no excuse for us as black men. We will adopt exploiting women, selling drugs and petty crimes as acceptable ways to make money like no one else does. Be honest. Our history of being

152

dehumanized is creating the desired and predictable effect, causing us to lose our own humanity. Each one of us needs to search our own souls and call ourselves on our ethics, morals, decency and humanity. We need to simultaneously determine what is, and what is not acceptable behavior for black men.

Bottom-up approach. Many of our organizations focus on working with those of us who are less in need than others. For example, regardless of how you feel about affirmative action, it is somewhat of an elitist program for our people. While it may help some of us enter college, obtain a job or promotion, it does <u>nothing</u> for young brothers and sisters who are being destroyed at an early age by the educational system or the criminal justice system. Those brothers and sisters may never get to a point where they can benefit from such a program. Our efforts need to target those of us who are most in need—the brother raising themselves because no one responsible is at home, the families that are known throughout the neighborhood as a breeding ground for the criminal mentality, the addicted, the violent and the young children struggling the most in school. Because we are missing the mark in this area, a huge class gap has developed between those of us who have a little something and those who don't.

Drugs & alcohol. As black men and boys we have to re-think our attitudes about drugs and alcohol. Although the earlier statistics we quoted state that blacks use drugs in proportion to our general number, and actually abuse alcohol at a lower rate than whites, there is still a huge problem. Drugs and/or alcohol were likely a contributing factor for most brothers involved in the criminal justice system—either by using, selling or both. Our collective attitude about drugs needs work. Smoking a blunt, drinking a forty and selling various drugs are too easily accepted by us as black men. We know that law enforcement concentrates most of their resources on us and our communities. We know that drugs and excessive alcohol are bad for your body and can negatively impact your life. We also know that chemicals of one form or another have been used as weapons against certain populations since America was stolen. Why then do we not take a long, hard look at our use in these areas? If we did so, it would damage the business of incarcerating us severely.

Domestic violence & sexual crimes. We need to stand up as black men to address domestic violence, sexual assault and sexual abuse. It needs to become an automatically known fact that black men and boys do not hit or verbally abuse women and girls. We need to talk about this, get this message out to each other, and offset the damage the media has helped create among us. Slapping women, calling them bitches and hoes, glamorizing the pimping, "playa" lifestyle, sexual assault and abuse are crimes that we must talk about and act upon among ourselves as black men. This will also decrease the number of us who come into contact with the criminal justice system. Every black community should have a group for black men struggling with domestic violence and anger issues. What is stopping us from starting such groups?

The social services business. When funding through local, state, or federal offices is available, the RFP (Request for Proposal), grant application or invitation to bid often involves at-risk populations. Often, these populations mean us. In other words, many are making money from our struggles. We need to insist—especially with local government— that these programs and local government Human Services Departments change the way they do business. We not only contribute to paying for these programs through our taxes, the proposals are written pertaining to us. Our values, cultural characteristics, strategies, and bodies need to be part of the process of addressing those issues in our communities. Rather than let others profit on our misery, we can be part of the solutions.

Working against ourselves. Many of our people who work in social services, law enforcement and criminal justice do little to ensure that the organizations they work for work in the best interests of our people and our communities. As Carter G. Woodson said, "How can I learn your song if I don't know my own?" Many of us, including those who work in these careers don't know who *we* are—our history, our problems or the solutions to them, so how can we better equip those institutions to do so. Many of our people in these fields have issues with internalized self-hatred; they have no desire to reach out to their own people. Still others (such as many police and correctional officers) are so hungry to be a part of the culture in which they work, they distance themselves from their own people.

Politics. For those of us who just can't help but to look externally for solutions to our problems, begin with the Democratic Party. For decades, we as black people have given our undying support and allegiance to a party that does little or nothing in return. We certainly aren't suggesting joining the Republican Party. What we are suggesting is putting elected officials—whatever their party affiliation—on the spot. What will their efforts be towards issues that truly plague our communities? Rather than vote for empty promises, we should have specific expectations of those that seek to become our elected officials.

Community-based solutions. We need to bring back the concept of dealing with the problems, and people who have problems, in our community within our communities. Either we are extremely passive and lethargic, or we are expecting external forces to address those problems of ours that we aren't even willing to address. This is psychological slavery where we refuse to cut the umbilical cord to our oppressors. Who would respect or help us when we show little willingness to help ourselves?

Criminal justice/sentencing reform. We do need to continue to work in this area, for many brothers who are being locked up for non-violent drug offenses actually belong in treatment. America scares the public to demand tougher sentencing laws by showing our faces. Getting elected officials to back off harsh sentencing will be tough, which is why we need to continue our internal healing so fewer brothers are entering the system to begin with. While re-defining black manhood, special efforts need to be made to reach out to the brothers who are deeply entrenched in illegal lifestyles, while at the same time pushing for services that will be of use for those exiting the institutions such as housing, cultural re-education/support and livable wage employment.

Work with our children. To break the chain of the cycle of black males accepting incarceration as a normal part of life, we need to work with the little brothers. We can offset the images of lost, older brothers such as 50 Cent, Lil John, Snoop and so many others the media intentionally bombards them with, and help them develop a self-determined image of black manhood. It's up to us.

154

CONCLUSION
(OR A NEW BEGINNING)

Thank you for taking the time to read and work through this book. Taking responsibility for your own healing and beginning the journey to reclaim a powerful place in this world is a commendable act. As with any self-help process, you'll get out of it what you put into it.

With a subject of this magnitude, inevitably there will be something left out. This book is no exception. There are a number of issues we did not adequately discuss, including:

Black Leadership:
We are a people who have often waited on a charismatic leader to tell us what to do and how to do it—and in many cases what to think. In our humble opinion, the concept of black leadership is outdated and ineffective. Rather than following a leader, it may be more effective for us to follow a theme - that of healing from our trauma and the subsequent redefinition, empowerment and unity that comes along with it. Besides, leadership tends to become self-serving, elitist and compromised. We are all capable (and in need) of being leaders as well as humble supporters.

Africa/African Immigrants & Refugees:
We have written extensively of our theft from the Motherland, the loss of our culture and the need for healing from such trauma. We have not written much about the issues— positive and negative—that are actually taking place in various parts of Africa. Part of our healing should be establishing real and meaningful connections to the people and issues affecting our brothers and sisters in Africa. A striking illustration of the gap that exists can be seen in the comparison of rock star Bono, leader of the group U2, and rapper Ludacris. While Bono has committed himself to saving the lives of Africans, Ludacris goes to Africa to make a rap video titled, "Pimpin' All Over the World." This blatantly shows how lost we are, and proves our need to redefine our values, before we can be of any benefit to our brothers and sisters back home.

As far as our recent brothers and sisters from Africa, we should extend ourselves to them unconditionally. Many have undergone trauma in their own land of origin, and we know that the media has often given them reason to fear us. They are often as unaware of our experiences as we are of theirs. Rather than ridiculing and marginalizing them, we should appreciate that which they have that we don't - a specific knowledge of where they come from and their cultural history, and learn about their history from them. It may even be your own history and culture you're learning.

Inter-racial Relations:
We are talking about how we, as black people, interact with other groups of people. As minorities in America, we often allow ourselves to be pitted against each other. As black people, we spend a great deal of time and energy resenting the economic gains of others (Mexican immigrants – documented or undocumented, Southeast Asians, African

immigrants and refugees). We should not "hate" on others because they have that which we lack—knowledge of who they are, where they come from, and the cultural bonds that allow them to work together. They do what we should be doing. For black Americans to resent their economic gains doesn't make us *look* petty, it *is* petty.

As for how other racial groups see us, we must understand that America's propaganda about us is promoted worldwide. Many in other countries have been given a negative perception of us long before they arrive in this country. We don't need to prove anything to them, but simply understand where their perceptions come from. Besides, respect is earned, not given. What do recent immigrants to America see us doing in our communities? Do they see us killing each other? Stealing from each other? Selling poison to each other? In many cases they do. Again, we have nothing to prove to others, but we can only hold others accountable for how they treat us, after we hold ourselves accountable for how we treat each other.

Those of us who routinely speak out against oppression need to decide if we are truly against the oppression of people, or simply want to be on the side of power when such oppression takes place. Too often, we remain silenced and watch instances of oppressive behaviors towards others, sometimes feeling relief that it "isn't us this time." Others battles for human rights must also be our battles. There is not a clearer example than with the plight of the proud Native American people. While many of us as blacks have Native blood in our veins, and while the indigenous (original) people of America have repeatedly had our backs throughout history, we have repeatedly ignored their oppression, and often contributed to it.

The Environment:
As people of African descent, and similar to our Native American brothers and sisters, we have historically seen ourselves as one with the earth. The concept of "conquering" nature (mountains, space, other civilizations) is a European concept. We originally lived as one with our environment. However, with our current distorted identity, we now hold the embarrassing position of the world's ultimate, materialistic consumers. We value gold and diamonds that often cost African children their freedom and lives. We sport mink and fur coats as a sign of status, oblivious to the barbaric treatment of animals whose lives were lost to feed our vanity. We roll in the most gas-guzzling, air-polluting automobiles. We sell and ingest many of nature's and man's most poisonous materials. Litter, broken bottles and environmental deterioration are often the marks of our communities.

Homophobia/Sexual Minorities:
Because of our community's historical relationship with Christianity, as well as our often-exaggerated definitions of black manhood, many of us tend to be extremely homophobic. While it is not our intent here to support or oppose the lifestyles of sexual minorities, we would do well to spend some time looking at our judgments of others. We don't want to fall into the trap of marginalizing others the way we have been as a way to make ourselves feel superior. It is a form of internalized self-hatred to treat others the way we have been treated. Our distorted sense of black manhood often results in passing judgment or questioning the manhood (or womanhood) of others based on our own distorted self-concept. In either case, as we undergo our own redefinition, it should result in a healthier, more compassionate and humanistic view of others.

We don't assume to have all of the answers for our people. As the saying goes, "There is nothing new under the sun." Many of the conversations happening within the covers of this book are happening in barbershops and living rooms around the country. But the truth remains: we've asked for reparations, restoration of our legal status, government aid programs, etc., but we have never taken an inventory of the trauma our history has caused us, and then taken the steps to heal from that trauma.

In order to be healthy, whole human beings, people who undergo other forms of trauma—sexual abuse, family violence, chemical dependency or war—a self-inventory and subsequent healing is essential. Why then, have we failed to see the need for our own healing, when all of these traumas, as well as others, have been a part of our history? Instead we pass the effects of that trauma from generation to generation.

It would also be a mistake to assume that this booklet can be of help only to those of our brothers who are most disenfranchised. Black men who are bankers, architects, entertainers, professional athletes, judges, law enforcement officers, politicians, military personnel, electricians, educators, salesmen and every other profession share one trait. That is, we all lack the inherent knowledge of who we are, where we come from and the ingrained self-concept of black manhood which that knowledge would provide. Therefore, most of us go through our daily pursuits without contributing anything to the collective benefit of our people. In fact, many of us with the professional status and financial means to help, do more damage than benefit to our people. To measure our success simply by our professional or financial status is, once again, someone else's definition of accomplishment. Considering our unique history, it is foolish for any of us not to recognize the hole that has been created in our souls.

So let our work begin. Many experts feel that America is crumbling around the edges. We export fewer goods while importing many. We are the most violent, perverted, polluting and materialistic nation in the world's history. Other societies view us as oppressive, dangerous warmongers willing to justify our actions by any means. We can continue to roll with this sinking ship, or, as Minister Louis Farrakhan said during the original Million Man March, "Black men not only have the ability to lead *America* to a higher level of consciousness, but also the *world*." Brothers, no other people have been the targets of the hate, fear and jealousy and that we have. Yet, here we are, still standing, the envy of the world.

Let the healing, redefinition and uplifting begin. Peace.

For Women Who Are Concerned
About the Plight of Black Males

Whether you are a mother, grandmother, aunt, wife, sister, girlfriend or other woman who loves, raises, or are otherwise concerned about black males, this is for you.

As we distributed the first edition of this book, we noticed something interesting, yet predictable. Brothers would look at it, talk about how good it was, and swear they were going to read it and take action on what was within the covers. Yet, it was the sisters who were the most passionate. In some instances, we thought the best way to get this book into the hands of the brothers and to get them involved in something was to go through black women.

This is a testament to your passion, strength, love and loyalty to us as black men. However, it doesn't speak well for us. This is why the book was written. We know we are often damaged goods. Part of the damage promotes complacency, passivity, individualism, oblivion and hopelessness.

As we stated in the book, black communities throughout America have become matriarchies, meaning basically that sister take care of most of the business. Brothers won't like hearing that, but simply looking at who is raising our children points this out more than any other statistic.

Therefore, as black men, we have some words of advice to women who love black boys and men:

Don't present a desperate, powerless, helpless image when seeking help raising your sons/grandsons.

> Children count on their parents/guardians as a safety net. Long after your son or grandson physically outgrows you, you are still that psychological safety net. You may be the one who gave birth to him, changed his diapers, dried his tears and fought for him. Whether they exhibit it or not, most of our young men know they are sometimes out of control, lost and confused. They count on you to provide stability. The last thing they need is to look to you and see powerlessness and helplessness.

> That doesn't mean you can't ask for help. As Na'im Akbar stated in his book, *Visions for Black Men*, all a sister should have to do is say she needs help and brothers should be there from church, neighborhood, family or place of employment.

> Black women (and the men who love them) should never again present the powerless victimization we often embrace as a people. There is not a greater model of strength, perseverance, determination and love than a black woman who knows who she is. Claim that power.

159

When raising your sons/grandsons, don't verbally/physically abuse them.

Truth is, some women do more damage to the boys in their care within the first 6 years of their lives than society will do in the next 20. Yelling, screaming, cussing out, belittling, and otherwise going off on children damages their self-esteem. 85% of the brain develops by age 5, and the thoughts formed during that time are lasting. We know that many of us are stressed out and disillusioned, but the cruelest thing of all is to take it out on our kids. It can severely retard their development and damage their self esteem.

Many of us believe this way of parenting is a cultural thing. Check the history of black parenting and you will find that this is a practice we learned during our traumatic time in America. Severe punishment or even death could await a black child who didn't obey immediately, especially black males. When you look at many different African cultures that are healthy and functional, the village concept doesn't require beating, verbally abusing and destroying the self esteem of their children.

I've often heard sisters say our children started going bad when "white people wouldn't let us whip 'em anymore." Our children don't need the threat of physical punishment to help them become strong and proud. They need love and guidance.

Work on your own issues, and then choose the brothers you interact with based on sound values.

We're not trying to be harsh, but how many sisters find brothers who work everyday, pay their bills and don't have the "Mack-Daddy" mentality boring? On the other hand, the same sisters get 'sprung' over the sharp, smooth, well dressed brother in the nice car who lies, is manipulative and has little substance. It's time to figure out what you consider a real man to be.

When you meet a man who has children he doesn't seem to be involved with, what makes you think he'll be a father to those you have with him? When you first meet a brother, what are you most interested in finding out about him? How smooth he is verbally, or whether he volunteers with some organization? Are you more concerned with the kind of car he drives, or how he sees himself as a black man? Are you more concerned with how much money he makes, or how he spends and invests the money he has? Are you more influenced by his ability to (as my mom used to say) "talk a hole in your head," or how honest he is with you about himself, his feelings, his goals and his priorities? Does he have kids of his own? If so, how does he treat them? If not, how does he treat his nephews and nieces? Does he give his time as a coach, tutor, mentor or Big Brother?

Sisters, as men, most of what we do is to influence and impress you all. If you come correct, look for noble traits within us, you'll find that you have more influence and power than you ever thought. But you have to know what a *true* black man is. Many sisters don't.

If you're raising a black boy, teach him to have a strong work ethic.

Like the saying goes, "Women raise their daughters and love their sons." From the time a black boy is old enough to do so, he should have tasks that are his responsibility to perform. These responsibilities can include taking out the garbage, raking leaves, cutting the grass, cleaning his room or other parts of the house and helping care for his siblings or elderly relatives.

However, don't make the mistake many sisters make of telling a boy, "You are the man of the family." He is not; he's a boy. He has no idea how to be a man. You need to teach him, and show him through your expectations and interactions with real men what a black man does and is. Don't make him take on responsibilities that are yours as his parent, such as raising your other children. He can assist with babysitting duties, but being the primary caregiver to your kids isn't his responsibility. You brought him into the world, not vise-versa.

Be mindful it you have a son or grandson who is in his upper teenage years who exhibits the following traits: If he doesn't want to go to school, won't work, always insists on the latest "gear," must have his hair perfectly coifed, and always expects money from you or other people, you are raising a boy.

Undergo your own healing process.

As black people, we all have been through an unprecedented traumatic experience for over 400 years. Take responsibility for your own healing process.

Hopefully, part of your healing will include looking at how you view black men, and any unresolved anger, hatred, resentment or hurt you have towards brothers. While our behavior has caused much of this, you likewise have been socialized *not* to respect and love brothers. We're not saying you don't, just that part of our trauma in America was/is to program us into looking at each other as adversaries.

We've placed an unfair burden on you. YOU are raising the majority of black boys. As black men we may be slow to step up to the plate, but in the meantime, you are the ones who give birth to, teach, and raise black boys. Take advantage of it in the way you raise our boys and the problem will improve.

Also, in various settings, don't say, "I'm a single parent." as if it is an affliction or disease. It is what it is, and isn't a disability that will give you special allowances. On the other hand, it isn't something to take pride in. All it says is that the father of your child/children either is deceased or is not taking his share of the responsibility for raising his kids. In some instances it also acts as a pre-emptive excuse not to raise your child in a responsible manner, to set your child up for your own expected failure. It is possible for a woman to raise a strong, proud black man. Women do it everyday.

Model healthy relationships

This goes back to undertaking your own healing process and having an understanding of who the black man is. If you don't do both, you may be at risk of getting involved in unhealthy relationships. Expecting strong relationships for yourself shows your expectations and family values, just as the opposite does. If boys (and girls) are exposed to relationships where there is arguing, cussing, crying, drama and violence, this traumatizes them. As they grow older they often repeat those patterns. Likewise if they see respectful exchanges between equal partners.

Sisters, all black men aren't dogs. If you are repeatedly mistreated by men (and exposing your children to it) it is time to look at yourself. Now, we're not saying that it is your fault that men hit or mistreat you. However, if you continue to get involved with one abusive relationship after another, the type of men you get involved with *is* your responsibility.

Show brothers respect/love

This doesn't mean letting us in your pants anytime we try to run some weak game. We're simply talking about acknowledging each other on the street, at work or in the community. There is a great deal of tension and hurt between black women and men, and there are certain, simple steps we can take to begin the healing.

When you see a black man or boy in public, smile and speak to us. Don't worry about us taking it the wrong way. If we do, correct us by saying something like; "My brother, I was simply acknowledging you as a black man. I have some understanding about how society looks at you and I don't share that feeling. I should be able to speak to you – black woman to black man – without it meaning I'm throwing you action." Unless he's an extremely ignorant and lost brother, he'll get it.

Besides, there is nothing in the world like a black woman's smile.

Check your materialism/consumerism

You are naturally beautiful. Don't max out your credit cards through blind consumerism. As a people, we may well be the most materialistic and some-what superficial on earth. Believe it or not, it hurts some of us black men to see you throwing yourselves at some simple-minded brother simply because he has money and other material objects.

The materialistic gold-digger isn't a myth. She is real, and there are some sisters who have no shame in stating their desire to use men for what we have. If this is your value, or you justify this belief, you should have no quarrel with pimps. They're both the same. Most importantly, this value sends a very negative message to our sons and daughters.

Some sisters rarely buy their small sons a book, yet have them decked out in the newest Jordans and name brand gear. This is a pattern that continues as your sons get older. They learn immediate gratification, superficial values and the "image above substance" value system.

As both black women and men, we need to start thinking about how, when and where we spend our money. Corporate America counts on ignorant, blind image spending. No one should respect us if we are so easily parted from our money.

Set limits with your sons, grandsons & partners

If you have a son, grandson, boyfriend, husband or other black man/boy in your life and he refuses to man up, don't be afraid to set limits with him. Your loving spirit is wonderful, but sometimes we need tough love. For the son/grandson who won't go to school or get a job? Give him a choice of doing so or getting his own place. And stick to it. For the boyfriends/husband who has every excuse as to why he can't get a job while you go to work everyday, give him the same choice.

Don't **ever** let a man hit you. If he does, call 9-1-1 on him. Don't fall for the okie-doke of "So, you gonna get the white man on me?" Until we as black men stand up and develop a strategy to deal with brothers among us who put their hands on women, you don't have much choice. Besides, brothers kill sisters regularly through domestic violence, and most of us don't seem to have the capacity to decide on our own accord that hitting women isn't OK.

If you feel your man is sexually inappropriate with your children, he very well may be. Don't be in denial. Do what you need to do to protect your children and yourself.

If your man or other family member is addicted to drugs and/or alcohol, he has to go to treatment or he has to go. Same thing if he sells drugs or engages in other illegal activity. If he cheats on you he has to go. As black men, we have done a pitiful job of developing an infrastructure to deal with our own problems. Until we do, you have to protect yourself.

You can continue to love a brother through his struggles, but he has to make some choices. You can try talking to him, getting other brothers to talk to him, praying for him and/or encouraging him to better himself, but at some point don't be afraid to make the difficult choices. You may be doing them a great favor.

Don't deny the father of your child the opportunity to be a father

Sometimes we as men and women use children – or financial support of our children – as a weapon against our ex. I know many brothers who won't get involved with their children or withhold financial support just to hurt the mother of those children. Some don't know this is their motive, but it is.

There are also times when women will deny the fathers of their children access to those children for various reasons: financial support, anger, resentment and revenge. If a man wants to be a father and doesn't put the child in any kind of danger, the mother should not deny him access to his children. It may sound hard, but the financial issues are the mother's concerns, not the child's. All that child may want is to be involved with their father. Maybe as this brother interacts with his child, it will come to him that part of being a father is physical, emotional AND financial support.

Bottom line: if he is a decent father, loves his child/children, has a safe environment for them and doesn't expose them to harm, don't be the reason he can't see his kids.

Encourage your son/grandson/boyfriend/brother/friend to get involved

Recently, Latino brothers and sisters organized by the hundreds of thousands across the country to advocate for immigration. It was a beautiful thing. It was reminiscent of the civil rights movement of the past.

It also pointed out the stark contrast among black men and how passive and complacent we've become. It has become extremely hard to get a large group of black men to engage in something positive. We have been trained to be preoccupied with the superficial and irrelevant. Sadly, when significant numbers of brothers do get together (concert, club, or sporting event) violence often breaks out.

Ironically, things are worse than ever for black boys and men when you consider the statistics. There has never been a time when we needed to be involved in social activism and organizing more than now.

Urge your son, grandson, brother, nephew, husband or other brothers you know to get involved with something – ANYTHING – that contributes to the betterment of our people. This should be a new standard by which by which brothers are judged: "What are you doing to help our people?"

We have so much work to do that we can ill afford to waste any more time. Let our healing begin – together.

For Our Young Brothers
(Especially for those young men under age 13)

Before you begin, it is very important that we—older black men—apologize to you younger brothers. In many ways we have failed you as fathers, teachers and protectors. Your idea of what a proud, positive black man is might be mixed up because WE have done a poor job of showing you by the way we live our lives.

We want to make up for that.

While this book was written because black boys and men older than you have some work to do, our biggest reason for writing it is to make a better place for you young brothers (and our sisters) to grow up. Also, we want you to have a better understanding of what being a strong, proud black man is.

If you are under 14 years old, try to read the whole book anyway. But this part is written especially for you.

Read the following questions and comments, write your answers down in the spaces provided, and think hard about what you write. If you need help, ask dad, mom, grandma, your older brother or sister or a teacher or coach. If it helps, you can tell them your big brothers Aaron and Larry said they should help you.

Do you like to read books?

If you do, congratulations. Keep reading. The most powerful thing in life you can do is exercise your mind. If you don't like to read, somebody is playing (fooling) you. Read anything: comic books, sports sections, even rap magazines. <u>Just read</u>!! As you learn to enjoy it and become better at it, hopefully you will start reading other things, like newspapers and books that help you understand yourself, your people, and the world you live in.

How much time each day do you spend watching TV, playing video games, and playing sports?

Other than what you <u>have</u> to do at school, how much time do you spend reading each day?

Sports and video games might be fun, but reading helps you think better. It improves your vocabulary (use of words) and writing skills. Better thinking skills also helps you figure out problems, avoid negative situations, and develop into your own person instead of trying to be like everybody else.

Did you know that for hundreds of years in this country it was against the law for black people to learn how to read or write? If a black person was caught trying to read or write, they could be beat or killed. Even young brothers like you. This is because there is power in the ability to read.

Ask yourself what sense does it make when black boys say, "I don't like to read." Are you letting someone fool you into not reading? If you don't do it, or don't like to do it, you are letting them 'play' you. Reading is something many people say black boys don't like to do, and don't do very well. Prove them wrong.

We are not telling you to stop doing all the fun things you like to do. But starting today, get a book that you like and sit down in a quiet place and read it. Start with just 15 minutes if you need to, but work until you can read for 1 hour or more at a time. We promise it will make a big difference in your life.

Do you like to watch TV, movies, and rap videos?

When you see someone who looks like you on TV, movies, or music videos, what are they usually doing?

If your answers were like ours, black boys and men are usually playing sports, in music videos, shown as criminals, or in shows where they are trying to make people laugh.

Look at the very beginning of this book and read about all the black inventors on the list. Everyday, you and just about every other person in the world uses something that a black person, or African, invented.

Then, why is it so hard for you to see a black scientist, architect (building designer) or inventor on TV?

At the same time, why is it so easy for you to see a black football player, basketball player, rapper, or comedian?

We think it is because the people who control the media (TV, movies, radio & music videos) know that you will try to do the things you see others that look like you do. These people want you to spend your time trying to be a basketball or football player, or a rapper. They don't want you to be a doctor, teacher, inventor, scientist, or the many other things you can be.

How would you feel if your mom or grandmother was doing the things women do on a 50 Cent, Snoop-Dogg or Lil John music video?

166

Then what do you think about other black women wearing hardly any clothes shaking their behinds on these videos?

Do you think its ok to treat black women like this?

Do you ever wonder why the people who control the media think its ok to show black men treating black women this way? Remember, it could be your grandmother, mother or sister dancing around like that.

Also, there are many positive, strong, proud black rappers who rap about things that will actually help you think and view things differently. Some of them are: Common, Kanye West, Talib Kweli, Dead Prez and many others. BET, MTV, VH-1 and Soul Train don't often show these rappers. It's almost as if the media only wants you to see the rappers who talk about nothing but partying, "bling-bling" and the gangster lifestyle.

Ask an older person like your grandparents to describe how black people were shown on TV when they were young. Write down some of the words they use.

Now, watch or have someone record (with your parent's permission) shows and movies like Jerry Springer, Maury Povich, any television court show, Yo Momma, Soul Plane, and most any music video. Carefully watch how the black people act on these shows and in the audience.

What did you notice?

You may have seen black people fighting, black men and women talking bad about each other for the world to see, black people doing stupid stuff to make people laugh, and black people yelling and laughing at each other as we make fools of ourselves. Did you notice any of these things?

Listen carefully. If you didn't notice these things and the shows just seemed funny to you, it might be because you are being taught to see black people as clowns, buffoons and ignorant people who won't be able to do much in life that is positive.

Illegal activity

Is there a part of your neighborhood where gang members ever hang out?

Have you ever been nervous about walking through that part of the neighborhood?

Have you ever seen drug dealers in your neighborhood selling drugs?

Has any man in your family ever been arrested, in jail, or in prison? Do you know the reasons?

Has any man in your family ever graduated from college?

In America, there are now more black men locked up in prison than there are in college. So don't feel bad if you know more family members who have gone to jail or prison than have graduated from college. What you need to ask yourself is: Do you spend more of your time and effort into preparing to go to college some day, or are you spending more time preparing to go to prison?

We want you to start thinking very carefully about how you see yourself as a young, black man. The media shows you many images of black men doing illegal and disrespectful things. They want you to believe, as 50 Cent says, that you should "get rich or die trying." The truth is, most people die (or go to prison trying). America also spends a lot more money locking black men up in jails or prisons than it does helping black men go to college. Our actions help make that possible.

Which direction do you think your daily actions are taking you?

You can do anything you want in life. You come from a people who have done many great things. Which direction you go depends on <u>you</u>.

School

When you are at school, have you ever noticed a difference between how white kids, Asian kids, Latino kids and black kids act?

After thinking about it honestly, what differences do you notice?

Many black adults don't like to talk about this because they think we are saying it is entirely their own fault when black kids don't do as well as others in school. We are not saying this. Remember what we said about the media? When you see people that look like you clowning, rapping, or playing sports over and over, it influences how much effort you put into other things – like school. Knowing that, you can identify many things that you can do differently to put yourself in a position to do well in school. That is your responsibility.

"Acting white"

Have you, or another black student at school, ever teased some other black student by calling them a nerd, geek, square or sucka because it seemed like they were "acting white?"

What was the person doing that caused others to make fun of them?

Have you, or another black person you know, ever teased other students this way because they did well in school?

Often, when a white, Latino, or Asian student uses the word "nigga," listens to rap, talks a lot of mess, tells "yo momma" jokes, gets in trouble at school, cusses, sags their pants or hangs out with black kids, we say that this person is "acting black."

In a way, this is saying that activities that may get you in trouble or make you look less intelligent are "black," while things that will help you do better in school and use your brain are "white." Remember, for hundreds of years in this country, it was illegal and dangerous for black people to try to learn how to read and write. America <u>wanted</u> black people to be uneducated.

Now, ask yourself: What sense does it make for some black kids to act dumb on purpose?

Why is it <u>not</u> cool or seen as "white" for some black kids to do well in school?

It seems kind of crazy, doesn't it?

Young brother, it is time to give serious thought to how you view yourself as a young, black man. **Do you realize that black people in America are the only group of people in the world who don't know where we come from?** This is important because a man's idea of what it means to be a man is based on what he brings from his original country or tribe. Japanese, Sudanese, Irish and all other people in America can have a connection to their original country if they choose to. As black people, we were made to forget those connections.

So, when you hear a Mexican, Cambodian, Ethiopian, Samoan, or any other person speaking in their native language, you should never laugh or make fun of them. They have a knowledge of their original home that was taken from black people.

169

It is much easier to convince someone that gang-bangin, not doing well in school, pimping or selling drugs is a part of their idea of manhood when they don't know who they are. As black men, we had our languages, customs, values and cultures taken from us when we were kidnapped and brought here from many parts of Africa 400 years ago. This is why it is more important for you than anyone else to think carefully about what you do, who you are, and how you define yourself.

WHAT EVERY YOUNG, BLACK MAN SHOULD KNOW

- Reading is one of the most powerful things you can do. Reading can teach you so much about the world, and there is special power in reading books about the history of black people.

- Do not trust the images you see of black men on TV or movies. The media will often show you images of black men that look good, but are not good for you. The images that <u>are</u> good for you are often hidden from you by the media.

- There is no such thing as "acting black." Black people are some of the most educated, proud, creative and smart people in the world. There is no certain way of dressing, talking, walking or acting that is black. That is up to each of us to decide for ourselves. Your original self-concept – as we said earlier – was stolen over 400 years ago. The images you see of black people were given to us and controlled by others. Don't fall for it.

- We must learn to respect all people. Since we have learned to disrespect ourselves, we have also lost respect for others. Finding ways to respect other people can help us feel better about who we are, too.

- This means doing things like treating our elders better. Hold the door for older people, give up your seat on the bus, don't cuss in front of them and don't argue with them. In most other countries around the world, the elders are seen as wise and given much respect. America is one of the only countries that doesn't respect elderly people.

- It also means treating girls and women with more respect. Boys and men who hit girls and women, call them bitches and hoes, try to pimp them, and view them as objects are not men. They are confused boys who don't know what being a man is. Even if girls try to fight, cuss at, or disrespect you, remember that REAL men don't disrespect them.

- Do the best you can in school. Put the time in. Study. Do your homework. Don't think that doing well in school isn't cool. Ask an older person what happened to the "cool" brothers they knew growing up. Many of them ended up "being cool" in jail, prison, or hanging out on the streets doing nothing of value for black people.

- Remember: for a black man, education isn't just what you do in school. It also includes knowing yourself, learning about your people, being able to figure out when you are being lied to and being able to think for yourself.

- Never, ever avoid hard work. Men know how to work hard for what they want. Boys expect to be given things without work—this might be by hustling, runnin' game, pimping or doing illegal things. When your parents ask you to do chores around the house, do them and do them the best you can. You are developing a "work ethic" (the ability to work hard) and it will help you for the rest of your life. The more you work, the better you are able to do get and keep jobs later in life. This can lead to higher pay as an adult.

- Stay away from drugs, alcohol and cigarettes. Would you put dirt in your food and eat it? That's what you do when you put these chemicals in your body. One secret you might not have ever known is that drugs and alcohol have been used as weapons against certain people in America. Alcohol was used against Native Americans, heroin and crack against blacks. Drugs are one of the weapons used to lock black men up and destroy black families.

- Don't be a "slave" to money, jewelry, the newest clothes or the nicest cars. Did you know that little African kids are killed while being forced to mine for some of the jewelry you see rappers wearing in their videos? Many of the rappers either don't know this or don't care because THEY are slaves to money. The companies that put out the advertisement on TV don't care about you at all. They just want your money. There is much more to life than money. When 50 Cent says "get rich, or die trying" he is showing that he is a slave to money, and wants you to be one too, so he can make money off you.

- Don't engage in illegal activity. It isn't cool, it isn't hard, and it isn't being a man. Its kind of a dumb thing to do. When a young man steals a car just to ride around for a little while, gets caught, gets locked up for a week, and has to report to the court for a year, is it worth it? Judges, prosecutors, parole & probation officers, jail/youth detention/prison guards, police and many others make a lot of money from the high numbers of black boys and men who get in legal trouble and locked up. There are those who make it look exciting to do illegal things. Don't be fooled.

Young brother, whoever gave this to you to read really cares for you. Listen to them. Again, read this book, answer the questions and think hard about yourself and what you answered. We care a lot about you young brothers and want you to live the kind of life you want to live. The problems that exist are not your fault. They have existed for over 400 years. But you are responsible for the choices you make.

You should be very proud to be a young black man. No other people have gone through what your people have, yet we still have made a great impact on the world. If you understand the game being run to try to get you to fail, you can succeed anyway.

Peace.

CORE ELEMENTS
In Reclaiming & Redefining Black Manhood

Integrity: 1.) Moral or ethical strength. 2.) the quality of being honest. 3.) The condition of being free from defect or flaws. 4.) The state of being entirely whole.
In-teg-ri-ty: 1.) an unimpaired condition: SOUNDNESS 2.) firm adherence to a code of moral or artistic values: INCORRUPTIBILITY 3.) the quality or state of being complete or undivided: COMPLETENESS see HONESTY

Courage: The quality of mind enabling one to face danger or hardship resolutely.
Cour-age: Mental or moral strength to venture, persevere, and withstand danger, fear, or difficulty. COURAGE, METTLE, SPIRIT, RESOLUTION, TENACITY mean mental or moral strength to resist opposition, danger, or hardship. COURAGE implies firmness of mind and will in the face of danger or extreme difficulty: METTLE suggests an ingrained capacity for meeting strain or difficulty with fortitude and resilience. SPIRIT also suggests a quality of temperament enabling one to hold one's own or keep up one's morale when opposed or threatened: RESOLUTION stresses firm determination to achieve one's end: TENACITY adds to RESOLUTION implications of stubborn persistence and unwillingness to admit defeat.

Compassion: Sympathetic, sad concern for someone in misfortune.
Com-pas-sion: To sympathise: sympathetic consciousness of others' distress together with a desire to alleviate it.

Conscious: Tending toward awareness and appreciation.
Con-scious: 1.) sharing another's knowledge or awareness of an inward state or outward fact 2.) perceiving, apprehending, or noticing with a degree of controlled thought or observation 3.) personally felt guilt 4.) capable of or marked by thought, will, design, or perception 5.) SELFCONSCIOUS 6.) having mental faculties undulled by sleep, faintness, or stupor 7.) done or acting with critical awareness (made a conscious effort to avoid the same mistakes) 8.) likely to notice, consider, or appraise, being concerned or interested, marked by strong feelings or notions.

Ethic: A principle of right or good conduct or a body of such principles.
Eth-ic: 1.) The discipline dealing with what is good and bad and with moral duty and obligation 2.) a set of moral principles or values, a theory or system of moral values, the principles of conduct governing an individual or a group.

Morals: A principle of right or good conduct or a body of such principles.
Mor-al: 1.) of or relating to principles of right and wrong in behavior, expressing or teaching a conception of right behavior, conforming to a standard of right behavior, sanctioned by or operative on one's conscience or ethical judgement, capable of right and wrong actions 2.) probable though

not proved 3.) having the effect of such on the mind, confidence, or will: MORAL, ETHICAL, VIRTUOUS, RIGHTEOUS, NOBLE mean conforming to a standard of what is right and good. MORAL implies conforming to a standard of what is right and good. MORAL implies conformity to established sanctioned codes or accepted notions of right and wrong, ETHICAL may suggest the involvement of more difficult or subtle questions or rightness, fairness, or equity: VIRTUOUS implies the possession or manifestation of moral eminence and freedom from anything petty, mean, or dubious in conduct and character.

Honesty: 1.) The quality of being honest; truthful. 2.) Moral or ethical strength.
Hon-es-ty: 1.) Chastity 2.) fairness and straightforwardness of conduct 3.) adherence to the facts - uprightness of character or action; implies a refusal to lie, steal, or deceive in any way; suggests an active or anxious regard for the standards of one's profession, calling, or position; implies trustworthiness and incorruptibility to a degree that one is incapable of being false to a trust, responsibility, or pledge; implies tried and proven honesty or integrity.

Humility: Lack of vanity or self-importance.
Hu-mil-i-ty: The quality or state of being humble.

From *Roget's Thesaurus* and *Webster's Ninth New Collegiate Dictionary.*

SOURCES
and Other Suggested Readings

1. Akbar, Na'im. *Visions for Black Men.* Mind Productions, 1992.
2. Churchill, Ward and VanderWall, Jim. *The COINTELPRO Papers.* Cambridge, MA: South End Press, 1990.
3. Davis, Angela Y. "Masked Racism: Reflections on the Prison Industrial Complex." *Color Lines.* Fall 1998
4. Ellison, Ralph. *Invisible Man.* New York: Random House, Inc., 1952.
5. Entman, Robert M & Rojecki, Andrew. *The Black Image in the White Mind.* Chicago: University of Chicago Press, 2001.
6. Franklin, Anderson J. *From Brotherhood to Manhood.* Hoboken, NJ: John Wiley and Sons, Inc., 2004.
7. Gatto, John Taylor. "Against School." *Harper's* September 2003
8. Goldberg, Eve and Evans, Linda. "The Prison Industrial Complex and the Global Economy." *prisonactivist.org*
9. Haley, Alex and Malcolm X. *The Autobiography of Malcolm X.* New York: Balantine Books (reprint edition), 1973.
10. hooks, bell. *Rock My Soul: Black People and Self-Esteem.* New York: Washington Square Press, 2003
11. Kozol, Jonathon. *Savage Inequalities.* New York: Harper Perennial, 1992.
12. Kunjufu, Jawanza. *Countering the Conspiracy to Destroy Black Boys.* African American Images, 1995.
13. Kunjufu, Jawanza. *Solutions for Black America.* African American Images, 2004.
14. Leary, Joy DeGruy. *Post Traumatic Slave Syndrome.* Uptone Press, 2005.
15. Loewen, James. Lies My Teacher Told Me. New York: Touchstone Books, 1995.
16. Lui, Meizhu. "Doubly Divided: The Racial Wealth Gap." Racial Wealth Divide Project, 2004.
17. Price, Geoff. "Understanding Capitalism Part I." Rationalrevolution.net
18. Stamper, Norman. *Breaking Rank.* New York: Nation Books, 2005.
19. Webb, Gary. "The Dark Alliance." San Jose Mercury News, August 22, 1996.
20. Welsing, Frances Cress. *The Isis Papers.* Third World Press, 1991.
21. West, Kanye. *College Dropout.* Roc-a-fella Records/Def Jam, 2004.
22. Wisely, Willie. "The Bottom Line: California's Prison Industry Authority." www.prisonactivist.org
23. Woodson, Carter G. *The Miseducation of the Negro.* Trenton, NJ: Africa World Press, 1990.
24. Zinn, Howard. A People's History of the United States. New York: Harper Perennial, 1980.
25. FairEconomy.org
26. RacialWealthDivide.org
27. PrisonSucks.org